The Art of Aging Well:

Self-help, Volume 6

Timothy Scott Phillips

Published by Arcane Horizons Publishing, 2024.

THE ART OF AGING WELL:

First edition. November 29, 2024.

Copyright © 2024 Timothy Scott Phillips.

ISBN: 979-8227003843

Written by Timothy Scott Phillips.

Table of Contents

To all those embracing the journey of aging with courage and grace—

May this book inspire you to nurture your mind, body, and spirit as you discover the beauty in every season of life.

And to my family and friends, whose wisdom, love, and resilience remind me daily that aging well is a gift to cherish—this is for you.

Chapter 1: Introduction to Aging Well

The Concept of Aging Gracefully

Aging is an inevitable part of life, but how we approach and experience it can vary greatly. The concept of aging gracefully involves accepting the natural progression of life with a positive and proactive attitude. It's about embracing the changes that come with age while maintaining a sense of dignity, purpose, and well-being.

Understanding Aging Gracefully:

AGING GRACEFULLY DOESN'T mean denying or fighting against the aging process. Instead, it involves recognizing and accepting the changes that come with age, and finding ways to thrive despite them. It's about focusing on the positive aspects of aging, such as the wisdom and experience gained over the years, and using them to live a fulfilling life.

Key Components of Aging Gracefully:

1. ACCEPTANCE:

Acceptance is the first step towards aging gracefully. This means acknowledging the changes that come with age, both physical and mental, and understanding that they are a natural part of life. Acceptance allows you to focus on what you can do to maintain and improve your quality of life, rather than dwelling on the inevitable changes.

2. Positive Attitude:

A positive attitude can significantly impact your aging experience. Maintaining an optimistic outlook on life, staying open to new experiences, and finding joy in everyday moments can enhance your overall well-being and help you age gracefully.

3. Adaptability:

Adaptability is essential for aging gracefully. As you age, you may encounter various challenges and changes in your health, lifestyle, and circumstances. Being adaptable means being willing to make adjustments and find new ways to enjoy life, despite any limitations or changes you may face.

4. Self-Care:

Prioritizing self-care is crucial for aging gracefully. This includes taking care of your physical health through regular exercise, a balanced diet, and adequate sleep. It also involves attending to your mental and emotional well-being by engaging in activities that bring you joy, practicing mindfulness, and seeking support when needed.

5. Lifelong Learning:

Embracing lifelong learning is another key component of aging gracefully. Staying intellectually engaged by pursuing new hobbies, learning new skills, and keeping your mind active can help maintain cognitive function and provide a sense of purpose and fulfillment.

Embracing the Changes:

AGING GRACEFULLY IS about embracing the changes that come with age and finding ways to continue living a meaningful and fulfilling life. This may involve redefining your sense of purpose, nurturing relationships, and focusing on what truly matters to you. By adopting a mindset of acceptance, positivity, adaptability, self-care, and lifelong learning, you can navigate the aging process with grace and resilience.

Overview of the Mind-Body-Spirit Connection

⸺

The mind-body-spirit connection is a holistic approach to understanding and enhancing overall well-being. It recognizes that our mental, physical, and spiritual health are interconnected and that nurturing each aspect can lead to a more balanced and fulfilling life, especially as we age.

Understanding the Mind-Body-Spirit Connection:

1. MIND:

The mind encompasses our thoughts, emotions, and mental processes. Mental health is crucial for overall well-being and involves managing stress, maintaining cognitive function, and fostering positive emotions. Practices such as mindfulness, meditation, and mental exercises can help keep the mind sharp and resilient.

2. Body:

The body refers to our physical health and well-being. Physical health is maintained through regular exercise, a balanced diet, adequate sleep, and preventive healthcare. Taking care of the body can improve energy levels, reduce the risk of chronic diseases, and enhance overall quality of life.

3. Spirit:

The spirit represents our sense of purpose, meaning, and connection to something greater than ourselves. Spiritual health can be nurtured through practices such as meditation, prayer, spending time in nature, and engaging in activities that align with your values and beliefs. Spiritual well-being provides a sense of inner peace, fulfillment, and resilience.

The Interconnectedness of Mind, Body, and Spirit:

THE MIND, BODY, AND spirit are deeply interconnected, and each aspect influences the others. For example, physical exercise can improve mental health by reducing stress and boosting mood. Similarly, mental well-being can enhance physical health by promoting healthy behaviors and reducing the risk of chronic diseases. Spiritual health can provide a sense of purpose and inner peace that supports both mental and physical well-being.

Benefits of Nurturing the Mind-Body-Spirit Connection:

1. IMPROVED OVERALL Health:

A holistic approach to health that includes nurturing the mind, body, and spirit can lead to improved overall health and well-being. By addressing all aspects of health, you can reduce the risk of chronic diseases, improve mental and emotional health, and enhance your quality of life.

2. Enhanced Resilience:

Nurturing the mind-body-spirit connection can enhance resilience and help you cope with the challenges and changes that come with aging. A strong sense of purpose, mental clarity, and physical vitality can provide the strength and resilience needed to navigate life's ups and downs.

3. Greater Fulfillment and Happiness:

A holistic approach to health can lead to greater fulfillment and happiness. By nurturing your mental, physical, and spiritual well-being, you can create a sense of balance and harmony that contributes to a fulfilling and joyful life.

Practical Ways to Nurture the Mind-Body-Spirit Connection:

1. MINDFULNESS AND Meditation:

Practicing mindfulness and meditation can help reduce stress, improve mental clarity, and enhance emotional well-being. Set aside time each day for mindfulness practices, such as deep breathing, guided meditation, or simply being present in the moment.

2. Regular Physical Activity:

Engage in regular physical activity that you enjoy, whether it's walking, yoga, dancing, or swimming. Exercise not only benefits physical health but also boosts mood and mental clarity.

3. Healthy Eating:

Maintain a balanced diet rich in fruits, vegetables, whole grains, lean proteins, and healthy fats. Proper nutrition supports physical health, energy levels, and cognitive function.

4. Social Connections:

Nurture relationships with family, friends, and your community. Social connections provide emotional support, reduce feelings of loneliness, and contribute to a sense of belonging.

5. Spiritual Practices:

Engage in spiritual practices that resonate with you, such as prayer, meditation, spending time in nature, or participating in religious or spiritual communities. These practices can provide a sense of inner peace and fulfillment.

Importance of a Holistic Approach to Aging

A holistic approach to aging recognizes the interconnectedness of the mind, body, and spirit and emphasizes the importance of nurturing each aspect to achieve overall well-being. This approach goes beyond simply addressing physical health and includes mental, emotional, and spiritual well-being.

Key Principles of a Holistic Approach to Aging:

1. INTEGRATIVE HEALTH:

Integrative health involves combining conventional medical treatments with complementary therapies to address the whole person. This approach recognizes that physical health is influenced by mental, emotional, and spiritual factors and aims to create a comprehensive plan for well-being.

2. Preventive Care:

Preventive care focuses on maintaining health and preventing disease through lifestyle choices, regular check-ups, and early detection. This includes a balanced diet, regular exercise, stress management, and preventive screenings.

3. Personalized Care:

Personalized care tailors health and wellness strategies to the individual's unique needs, preferences, and goals. This approach recognizes that each person's aging experience is different and requires a customized plan for optimal well-being.

4. Lifelong Learning:

Lifelong learning emphasizes the importance of continuous personal and intellectual growth. Engaging in new hobbies, learning new skills, and staying mentally active contribute to cognitive health and a sense of purpose.

5. Community and Social Connections:

Maintaining strong social connections and being part of a community are essential for emotional well-being. Social support provides a sense of belonging, reduces feelings of loneliness, and enhances overall quality of life.

Benefits of a Holistic Approach to Aging:

1. COMPREHENSIVE WELL-Being:

A holistic approach to aging addresses all aspects of health, leading to comprehensive well-being. By nurturing the mind, body, and spirit, you can achieve a balanced and fulfilling life.

2. Improved Quality of Life:

Focusing on all aspects of health can improve your overall quality of life. Physical vitality, mental clarity, emotional stability, and spiritual fulfillment contribute to a sense of well-being and happiness.

3. Enhanced Resilience:

A holistic approach can enhance resilience and help you cope with the challenges of aging. A strong sense of purpose, mental strength, and physical health provide the foundation for navigating life's changes with confidence.

4. Greater Longevity:

Adopting healthy lifestyle choices and preventive care can contribute to greater longevity. By addressing all aspects of health, you can reduce the risk of chronic diseases and enjoy a longer, healthier life.

Practical Strategies for Adopting a Holistic Approach to Aging:

1. REGULAR EXERCISE:

Engage in regular physical activity that you enjoy. Exercise supports physical health, boosts mood, and enhances cognitive function. Aim for a mix of aerobic, strength training, and flexibility exercises.

2. Balanced Diet:

Maintain a balanced diet that includes a variety of nutrient-rich foods. Focus on whole foods, such as fruits, vegetables, whole grains, lean proteins, and healthy fats. Proper nutrition supports physical and mental health.

3. Mental Stimulation:

Keep your mind active by engaging in intellectually stimulating activities. Read books, solve puzzles, learn new skills, or take up a new hobby. Mental stimulation enhances cognitive function and provides a sense of accomplishment.

4. Stress Management:

Practice stress management techniques, such as mindfulness, meditation, deep breathing, and relaxation exercises. Managing stress supports emotional well-being and reduces the risk of chronic diseases.

5. Social Connections:

Maintain and nurture relationships with family, friends, and your community. Social connections provide emotional support, reduce feelings of loneliness, and enhance overall well-being.

6. Spiritual Practices:

Engage in spiritual practices that resonate with you. This may include meditation, prayer, spending time in nature, or participating in religious or spiritual communities. Spiritual practices provide a sense of inner peace and fulfillment.

7. Preventive Healthcare:

Schedule regular check-ups and preventive screenings to maintain your health. Early detection and intervention can prevent or manage chronic diseases and enhance your quality of life.

8. Lifelong Learning:

Embrace a mindset of lifelong learning. Pursue new hobbies, take courses, attend workshops, and engage in activities that challenge and stimulate your mind. Lifelong learning supports cognitive health and personal growth.

9. Self-Care:

Prioritize self-care by taking time for activities that bring you joy and relaxation. This may include hobbies, spending time with loved ones, or simply enjoying quiet moments. Self-care supports emotional and mental well-being.

Case Studies: Holistic Approach to Aging Well

Case Study 1: Jane's Journey to Holistic Health

JANE, A 68-YEAR-OLD retiree, realized that her sedentary lifestyle and poor eating habits were taking a toll on her health. Determined to make positive changes, she adopted a holistic approach to aging well.

Jane's Strategies:

- EXERCISE: JANE STARTED walking daily and joined a local yoga class. She found that regular exercise improved her energy levels and mood.

- Diet: Jane consulted a nutritionist and revamped her diet to include more fruits, vegetables, and whole grains. She noticed improvements in her digestion and overall well-being.

- Mental Stimulation: Jane began attending community classes and took up painting as a new hobby. These activities kept her mind active and provided a sense of accomplishment.

- Social Connections: Jane reconnected with old friends and joined a local book club. Social interactions reduced her feelings of loneliness and provided emotional support.

- Spiritual Practices: Jane started a daily meditation practice and spent more time in nature. These practices brought her a sense of inner peace and fulfillment.

Results:

Through her holistic approach, Jane experienced significant improvements in her physical health, mental clarity, and emotional well-being. She felt more energetic, engaged, and connected to her community. Jane's journey highlighted the transformative power of a holistic approach to aging well.

Case Study 2: Robert's Path to Balance and Fulfillment

ROBERT, A 72-YEAR-OLD retired engineer, felt that his life lacked balance and purpose after retiring. He decided to adopt a holistic approach to find fulfillment in his later years.

Robert's Strategies:

- EXERCISE: ROBERT JOINED a local gym and started swimming regularly. Physical activity helped him maintain his fitness and boost his mood.

- Diet: Robert focused on eating a balanced diet rich in whole foods. He also learned to cook new healthy recipes, which he enjoyed sharing with friends.

- Mental Stimulation: Robert took up woodworking and joined a local workshop. The new hobby kept his mind engaged and provided a creative outlet.

- Social Connections: Robert volunteered at a local community center and participated in social events. Volunteering gave him a sense of purpose and connected him with like-minded individuals.

- Spiritual Practices: Robert explored mindfulness practices and attended meditation retreats. These practices helped him find inner peace and a deeper sense of meaning.

Results:

By adopting a holistic approach, Robert found balance and fulfillment in his later years. He maintained his physical health, developed new skills, and built meaningful relationships. Robert's experience demonstrated how a holistic approach can lead to a fulfilling and purposeful life.

Conclusion

Aging well involves more than just maintaining physical health; it requires a holistic approach that nurtures the mind, body, and spirit. By embracing the concept of aging gracefully, understanding the mind-body-spirit connection, and adopting a holistic approach to well-being, you can create a balanced and fulfilling life as you age.

In this chapter, we explored the importance of aging gracefully, the interconnectedness of the mind, body, and spirit, and practical strategies for adopting a holistic approach to aging. By integrating these principles into your daily life, you can enhance your overall well-being, build resilience, and enjoy a fulfilling and joyful journey through the aging process.

As you continue to explore the strategies for mind, body, and spirit outlined in this book, remember that aging is a natural and beautiful part of life. Embrace it with a positive attitude, stay open to growth and change, and nurture your mind, body, and spirit to live your best life at any age.

Chapter 2: Embracing the Aging Process

Changing Perceptions of Aging

Aging is a natural part of life, yet societal perceptions often cast it in a negative light. Many cultures emphasize youth, vitality, and physical beauty, creating a stigma around growing older. However, shifting our perceptions of aging can lead to a more fulfilling and enriched experience in our later years.

Understanding Societal Perceptions:

SOCIETY FREQUENTLY views aging through a lens of decline, focusing on physical deterioration, loss of independence, and reduced social relevance. Media representations often reinforce these stereotypes, portraying older adults as frail, dependent, or out of touch. These negative perceptions can contribute to ageism, both in societal attitudes and self-perception among older adults.

The Impact of Negative Perceptions:

NEGATIVE PERCEPTIONS of aging can have significant consequences:

1. Self-Esteem and Identity: Older adults who internalize negative stereotypes may struggle with self-esteem and a sense of identity. They may feel devalued or invisible, impacting their mental and emotional well-being.

2. Health and Well-Being: Research shows that negative attitudes toward aging can affect physical health. Individuals with negative self-perceptions of aging may experience worse health outcomes, including increased risk of cardiovascular disease and cognitive decline.

3. Social Isolation: Ageism can lead to social isolation, as older adults may withdraw from activities or feel excluded from social circles. This isolation can exacerbate feelings of loneliness and depression.

Changing Perceptions of Aging:

1. Celebrating Aging:

CHANGING PERCEPTIONS begins with celebrating the positive aspects of aging. Older adults possess a wealth of knowledge, experience, and wisdom that can be invaluable to society. By focusing on the strengths and contributions of older adults, we can shift the narrative from decline to celebration.

Steps to Celebrate Aging:

- HIGHLIGHT ACHIEVEMENTS: Recognize and celebrate the achievements of older adults in various fields, from work and community service to personal hobbies and interests.

- Share Stories: Share inspiring stories of older adults who have made significant contributions or overcome challenges. These stories can provide positive role models and counteract negative stereotypes.

- Promote Intergenerational Connections: Encourage interactions between generations to foster mutual respect and understanding. Intergenerational activities can highlight the value and contributions of older adults.

2. Redefining Beauty and Vitality:

REDEFINING BEAUTY AND vitality to include all ages is crucial for changing perceptions of aging. Society's narrow definition of beauty often excludes older adults, leading to a devaluation of their appearance and worth.

Steps to Redefine Beauty and Vitality:

- INCLUSIVE MEDIA REPRESENTATION: Advocate for diverse and realistic portrayals of older adults in media. Representation that showcases older adults as vibrant, active, and engaged can challenge stereotypes.

- Celebrate Natural Aging: Embrace and celebrate the natural aging process, including physical changes like wrinkles and gray hair. Promote the idea that beauty is not limited to youth but can be found at every age.

- Promote Healthy Aging: Emphasize that vitality is not solely about physical appearance but includes overall well-being. Encourage healthy lifestyles that support physical, mental, and emotional health at every age.

3. Educating and Raising Awareness:

EDUCATION AND AWARENESS are essential for changing perceptions of aging. By understanding the realities of aging and the contributions of older adults, society can develop a more balanced and respectful view.

Steps to Educate and Raise Awareness:

- PUBLIC EDUCATION CAMPAIGNS: Implement public education campaigns that highlight the benefits and opportunities of aging. Use media, workshops, and community events to share accurate information.

- Age-Friendly Policies: Advocate for age-friendly policies and practices in workplaces, communities, and institutions. Policies that promote inclusivity and accessibility can enhance the quality of life for older adults.

- Challenge Ageism: Encourage individuals to challenge ageist attitudes and behaviors. Provide resources and training to help people recognize and address ageism in their personal and professional lives.

Cultivating a Positive Mindset About Growing Older

Cultivating a positive mindset about growing older is a powerful tool for enhancing well-being and enjoying a fulfilling life. A positive attitude can influence how we experience aging, impacting our health, happiness, and overall quality of life.

The Benefits of a Positive Mindset:

1. ENHANCED WELL-BEING: A positive mindset can improve mental and emotional well-being, reducing feelings of anxiety, depression, and stress.

2. Better Health Outcomes: Research shows that individuals with a positive attitude toward aging tend to have better physical health, including lower risk of chronic diseases and longer life expectancy.

3. Increased Resilience: A positive mindset can enhance resilience, helping individuals cope with challenges and adapt to changes that come with aging.

4. Greater Life Satisfaction: Embracing aging with a positive attitude can lead to greater life satisfaction and a sense of purpose and fulfillment.

Steps to Cultivate a Positive Mindset:

1. Practice Gratitude:

GRATITUDE IS A POWERFUL practice that can shift your focus from what you lack to what you have. Regularly acknowledging and appreciating the positive aspects of your life can enhance your overall well-being and foster a positive outlook on aging.

Steps to Practice Gratitude:

- GRATITUDE JOURNALING: Keep a gratitude journal where you write down things you are thankful for each day. This practice can help you focus on positive experiences and cultivate a sense of appreciation.

- Express Gratitude: Take time to express gratitude to others. Whether through a thank-you note, a phone call, or a simple verbal acknowledgment, expressing gratitude can strengthen your relationships and enhance your sense of connection.

- Reflect on Positive Experiences: Regularly reflect on positive experiences and moments of joy. This reflection can reinforce positive memories and create a more optimistic outlook.

2. Focus on Strengths and Accomplishments:

FOCUSING ON YOUR STRENGTHS and accomplishments can boost your self-esteem and confidence. Recognizing your capabilities and achievements can help you embrace aging with a sense of pride and fulfillment.

Steps to Focus on Strengths and Accomplishments:

- IDENTIFY STRENGTHS: Take time to identify your strengths and talents. Reflect on past experiences where you demonstrated resilience, creativity, or leadership.

- Celebrate Achievements: Celebrate your accomplishments, both big and small. Recognize the effort and dedication that contributed to your successes.

- Set New Goals: Set new goals and challenges that align with your strengths and interests. Pursuing meaningful goals can provide a sense of purpose and motivation.

3. Embrace Lifelong Learning:

LIFELONG LEARNING IS a key component of a positive mindset about aging. Staying intellectually engaged and curious can enhance cognitive function, provide a sense of purpose, and foster a positive outlook.

Steps to Embrace Lifelong Learning:

- PURSUE HOBBIES AND Interests: Engage in hobbies and activities that interest you. Whether it's learning a new language, taking up a musical instrument, or exploring a new craft, pursuing interests can keep your mind active and engaged.

- Take Courses and Workshops: Enroll in courses and workshops that align with your interests and goals. Many community centers, universities, and online platforms offer opportunities for continued learning.

- Stay Curious: Cultivate a sense of curiosity and openness to new experiences. Approach each day with a willingness to learn and explore.

4. Foster Social Connections:

STRONG SOCIAL CONNECTIONS are essential for a positive mindset and overall well-being. Building and maintaining relationships can provide emotional support, reduce feelings of loneliness, and enhance your sense of belonging.

Steps to Foster Social Connections:

- STAY CONNECTED: MAKE an effort to stay connected with family, friends, and community. Regular communication, whether in person, over the phone, or through virtual means, can strengthen your relationships.

- Join Social Groups: Join social groups, clubs, or organizations that align with your interests. Participating in group activities can provide opportunities for social interaction and connection.

- Volunteer: Volunteering is a meaningful way to connect with others and contribute to your community. Volunteering can provide a sense of purpose and fulfillment while building social connections.

5. Practice Self-Compassion:

SELF-COMPASSION INVOLVES treating yourself with kindness, understanding, and acceptance, especially during challenging times. Practicing self-compassion can enhance your emotional well-being and help you navigate the aging process with grace.

Steps to Practice Self-Compassion:

- BE KIND TO YOURSELF: Treat yourself with the same kindness and understanding that you would offer to a friend. Avoid self-criticism and negative self-talk.

- Acknowledge Your Feelings: Acknowledge and validate your feelings, whether they are positive or negative. Allow yourself to experience and process your emotions without judgment.

- Practice Mindfulness: Mindfulness involves being present in the moment and accepting your experiences without judgment. Mindfulness practices, such as meditation and deep breathing, can enhance self-compassion and emotional well-being.

The Power of Acceptance and Gratitude

Acceptance and gratitude are powerful practices that can transform your experience of aging. Embracing acceptance and cultivating gratitude can enhance your well-being, foster resilience, and create a more fulfilling and joyful life.

Understanding Acceptance:

ACCEPTANCE INVOLVES acknowledging and embracing the reality of your experiences, including the changes and challenges that come with aging. Acceptance is not about giving up or resigning yourself to circumstances but about finding peace and contentment in the present moment.

The Benefits of Acceptance:

1. REDUCED STRESS AND Anxiety: Acceptance can reduce stress and anxiety by helping you let go of resistance and negative judgments about your experiences.

2. Enhanced Emotional Well-Being: Embracing acceptance can improve emotional well-being by fostering a sense of inner peace and contentment.

3. Increased Resilience: Acceptance can enhance resilience by helping you adapt to changes and challenges with grace and equanimity.

4. Improved Relationships: Acceptance can improve relationships by fostering empathy, understanding, and compassion for yourself and others.

Steps to Practice Acceptance:

1. Acknowledge Your Reality:

ACCEPTANCE BEGINS WITH acknowledging your reality, including the changes and challenges you may face. By acknowledging your experiences without judgment, you can begin to find peace and contentment in the present moment.

Steps to Acknowledge Your Reality:

- OBSERVE WITHOUT JUDGMENT: Observe your experiences and feelings without judgment. Notice any resistance or negative thoughts and gently let them go.

- Practice Mindfulness: Mindfulness can help you stay present and aware of your experiences. Engage in mindfulness practices, such as meditation, deep breathing, or simply being present in the moment.

- Reflect on Your Journey: Reflect on your life journey and the experiences that have shaped you. Acknowledge the changes and challenges you have encountered and the resilience you have demonstrated.

2. Embrace Impermanence:

ACCEPTANCE INVOLVES embracing the impermanent nature of life. Recognize that change is a natural part of life and that each moment is an opportunity for growth and transformation.

Steps to Embrace Impermanence:

- FOCUS ON THE PRESENT: Focus on the present moment and appreciate the experiences and opportunities it offers. Let go of worries about the past or future.

- Find Meaning in Change: Find meaning and purpose in the changes and challenges you encounter. Reflect on how these experiences contribute to your personal growth and development.

- Cultivate Flexibility: Cultivate flexibility and adaptability in the face of change. Embrace new experiences and opportunities with an open mind and heart.

3. Let Go of Control:

ACCEPTANCE INVOLVES letting go of the need to control every aspect of your life. Recognize that some things are beyond your control and focus on what you can influence.

Steps to Let Go of Control:

- IDENTIFY WHAT YOU Can Control: Identify the aspects of your life that you can influence and take positive action in these areas. For example, you can control your responses to situations, your self-care practices, and your attitudes.

- Release What You Can't Control: Acknowledge the aspects of your life that are beyond your control and release your attachment to them. Practice letting go of the need to control outcomes and trust in the natural flow of life.

- Practice Acceptance Statements: Use acceptance statements to reinforce your practice. For example, "I accept the changes that come with aging and embrace each moment as an opportunity for growth."

Understanding Gratitude:

GRATITUDE INVOLVES recognizing and appreciating the positive aspects of your life. Cultivating gratitude can enhance your overall well-being, foster a positive mindset, and create a sense of abundance and fulfillment.

The Benefits of Gratitude:

1. ENHANCED EMOTIONAL Well-Being: Gratitude can improve emotional well-being by fostering positive emotions and reducing feelings of anxiety and depression.

2. Improved Physical Health: Research shows that gratitude can have positive effects on physical health, including better sleep, lower blood pressure, and a stronger immune system.

3. Stronger Relationships: Expressing gratitude can strengthen relationships by fostering feelings of connection, appreciation, and trust.

4. Increased Resilience: Gratitude can enhance resilience by helping you focus on the positive aspects of your life and find meaning in challenges.

Steps to Cultivate Gratitude:

1. Practice Daily Gratitude:

MAKE GRATITUDE A DAILY practice by setting aside time each day to reflect on the things you are thankful for. This practice can shift your focus from what you lack to what you have, fostering a sense of appreciation and contentment.

Steps to Practice Daily Gratitude:

- GRATITUDE JOURNALING: Keep a gratitude journal where you write down three to five things you are grateful for each day. This practice can help you focus on positive experiences and cultivate a sense of appreciation.

- Morning or Evening Reflection: Set aside time each morning or evening to reflect on the things you are thankful for. This can be a quiet moment of reflection or a part of your meditation practice.

- Gratitude Rituals: Create gratitude rituals that you can incorporate into your daily routine. For example, take a moment before each meal to express gratitude for the food you are about to eat.

2. Express Gratitude to Others:

EXPRESSING GRATITUDE to others can strengthen your relationships and create a sense of connection and appreciation. Take time to acknowledge and thank the people who have made a positive impact on your life.

Steps to Express Gratitude to Others:

- THANK-YOU NOTES: WRITE thank-you notes to express your appreciation to friends, family members, or colleagues. A handwritten note can be a meaningful and personal way to convey your gratitude.

- Verbal Acknowledgment: Take opportunities to verbally acknowledge and thank others for their kindness and support. A simple "thank you" can go a long way in fostering positive relationships.

- Acts of Kindness: Show your gratitude through acts of kindness. Whether it's offering a helping hand, sharing a thoughtful gift, or providing support, acts of kindness can strengthen your connections and express your appreciation.

3. Reflect on Positive Experiences:

REGULARLY REFLECT ON positive experiences and moments of joy. This reflection can reinforce positive memories and create a more optimistic outlook.

Steps to Reflect on Positive Experiences:

- RECALL POSITIVE MOMENTS: Take time to recall positive moments and experiences from your day, week, or life. Reflect on the emotions and feelings associated with these moments.

- Share Positive Experiences: Share positive experiences with others. Discussing positive moments with friends or family can enhance your sense of joy and connection.

- Create a Gratitude Jar: Create a gratitude jar where you can write down positive experiences and moments of gratitude on slips of paper. Over time, the jar will fill with positive memories that you can revisit whenever you need a boost of gratitude.

4. Find Gratitude in Challenges:

FINDING GRATITUDE IN challenges can help you reframe difficult experiences and find meaning in adversity. Reflect on the lessons and growth that challenges have brought into your life.

Steps to Find Gratitude in Challenges:

- REFRAME CHALLENGES: Reframe challenges as opportunities for growth and learning. Reflect on how difficult experiences have contributed to your personal development and resilience.

- Identify Silver Linings: Identify the positive aspects or silver linings in challenging situations. Consider what you have learned, how you have grown, and the strengths you have developed.

- Practice Gratitude Statements: Use gratitude statements to reinforce your practice. For example, "I am grateful for the lessons and growth that challenges bring into my life."

Case Studies: Embracing the Aging Process

Case Study 1: Maria's Journey to Acceptance and Gratitude

Maria, a 70-year-old retiree, struggled with feelings of loss and frustration as she faced the physical changes and limitations that came with aging. Determined to embrace the aging process, Maria decided to focus on acceptance and gratitude.

Maria's Strategies:

- DAILY GRATITUDE PRACTICE: Maria started a daily gratitude journal, writing down three things she was grateful for each day. This practice helped her focus on positive experiences and foster a sense of appreciation.

- Mindfulness Meditation: Maria incorporated mindfulness meditation into her daily routine. She practiced being present in the moment and accepting her experiences without judgment.

- Reframing Challenges: Maria worked on reframing challenges as opportunities for growth. She reflected on the lessons and strengths she had gained from difficult experiences.

- Expressing Gratitude: Maria made an effort to express gratitude to others. She wrote thank-you notes to friends and family members, acknowledging their kindness and support.

Results:

Through her practice of acceptance and gratitude, Maria experienced significant improvements in her emotional well-being and overall outlook on life. She felt more content, resilient, and connected to others. Maria's journey highlighted the transformative power of acceptance and gratitude in embracing the aging process.

Case Study 2: John's Path to a Positive Mindset

JOHN, A 68-YEAR-OLD retired teacher, felt overwhelmed by the negative stereotypes and societal perceptions of aging. He decided to cultivate a positive mindset to enhance his well-being and enjoy a fulfilling life.

John's Strategies:

- LIFELONG LEARNING: John pursued new hobbies and interests, including learning to play the guitar and taking up gardening. These activities kept his mind active and provided a sense of purpose.

- Celebrating Achievements: John took time to celebrate his achievements, both big and small. He recognized the effort and dedication that contributed to his successes and felt a sense of pride.

- Social Connections: John joined a local community center and participated in social groups and activities. Building and maintaining relationships provided emotional support and reduced feelings of loneliness.

- Positive Affirmations: John used positive affirmations to reinforce his mindset. He repeated affirmations such as "I embrace aging with positivity and resilience" and "I find joy and fulfillment in every stage of life."

Results:

By cultivating a positive mindset, John experienced greater well-being, resilience, and life satisfaction. He felt more confident, engaged, and fulfilled in his daily life. John's path demonstrated how a positive mindset can transform the experience of aging.

Conclusion

Embracing the aging process involves changing perceptions of aging, cultivating a positive mindset, and harnessing the power of acceptance and gratitude. By shifting societal attitudes, celebrating the strengths and contributions of older adults, and fostering a positive outlook, we can create a more fulfilling and enriched experience of aging.

In this chapter, we explored the importance of changing perceptions of aging, practical steps to cultivate a positive mindset, and the transformative power of acceptance and gratitude. By integrating these practices into your daily life, you can enhance your overall well-being, build resilience, and enjoy a fulfilling and joyful journey through the aging process.

As you continue to explore the strategies for mind, body, and spirit outlined in this book, remember that aging is a natural and beautiful part of life. Embrace it with a positive attitude, stay open to growth and change, and nurture your mind, body, and spirit to live your best life at any age.

Chapter 3: Physical Health and Wellness

Importance of Regular Physical Activity

Physical activity is essential for maintaining overall health and wellness, especially as we age. Regular exercise helps improve physical fitness, boosts mood, enhances cognitive function, and reduces the risk of chronic diseases. It is a cornerstone of aging well, contributing significantly to the quality of life in older adults.

Benefits of Regular Physical Activity:

1. IMPROVED CARDIOVASCULAR Health:

Regular exercise strengthens the heart and improves circulation. It helps lower blood pressure, reduces bad cholesterol (LDL), and increases good cholesterol (HDL), thus decreasing the risk of heart disease and stroke.

2. Enhanced Muscular Strength and Flexibility:

Physical activity helps maintain muscle mass and strength, which are crucial for mobility and independence. Strength training exercises, in particular, can enhance muscle tone, improve balance, and reduce the risk of falls.

3. Bone Health:

Weight-bearing exercises, such as walking, jogging, and resistance training, are essential for maintaining bone density and reducing the risk of osteoporosis. Strong bones support overall mobility and prevent fractures.

4. Weight Management:

Regular physical activity helps manage body weight by burning calories and increasing metabolism. Maintaining a healthy weight reduces the risk of various health conditions, including diabetes and heart disease.

5. Improved Mental Health:

Exercise is known to boost mood and reduce symptoms of depression and anxiety. Physical activity stimulates the production of endorphins, the body's natural mood elevators, and helps alleviate stress.

6. Cognitive Function:

Regular exercise has been linked to improved cognitive function and a reduced risk of cognitive decline and dementia. Physical activity increases blood flow to the brain, supporting brain health and enhancing memory and thinking skills.

7. Better Sleep:

Physical activity can improve sleep quality by helping you fall asleep faster and enjoy deeper sleep. Regular exercise also helps regulate your sleep-wake cycle.

8. Increased Energy Levels:

Regular physical activity boosts energy levels by improving cardiovascular health and enhancing muscular strength. It helps you feel more energetic and capable of performing daily activities.

Types of Physical Activity:

1. AEROBIC EXERCISE:

Aerobic exercises, also known as cardiovascular or endurance exercises, are activities that increase your heart rate and breathing. Examples include walking, jogging, swimming, cycling, and dancing. Aim for at least 150 minutes of moderate-intensity aerobic exercise per week.

2. Strength Training:

Strength training exercises involve using resistance to build and maintain muscle mass and strength. Examples include lifting weights, using resistance bands, and bodyweight exercises such as push-ups and squats. Aim to include strength training exercises at least two days per week.

3. Flexibility Exercises:

Flexibility exercises help maintain the range of motion in your joints and muscles. Examples include stretching, yoga, and Pilates. Incorporate flexibility exercises into your routine several times per week to improve mobility and prevent stiffness.

4. Balance Exercises:

Balance exercises help improve stability and reduce the risk of falls. Examples include standing on one leg, heel-to-toe walking, and tai chi. Aim to include balance exercises at least two to three times per week.

Creating a Balanced Exercise Routine:

1. CONSULT YOUR HEALTHCARE Provider:

Before starting any new exercise routine, consult your healthcare provider, especially if you have any pre-existing health conditions or concerns. Your healthcare provider can help you design a safe and effective exercise plan tailored to your needs.

2. Set Realistic Goals:

Set realistic and achievable fitness goals based on your current fitness level and desired outcomes. Start with small, manageable steps and gradually increase the intensity and duration of your workouts.

3. Include a Variety of Exercises:

Incorporate a variety of exercises into your routine to address different aspects of fitness, including aerobic, strength, flexibility, and balance exercises. This variety can help prevent boredom and keep you motivated.

4. Listen to Your Body:

Pay attention to how your body responds to exercise. If you experience pain, dizziness, or shortness of breath, stop exercising and seek medical advice. It's important to exercise within your limits and avoid overexertion.

5. Stay Consistent:

Consistency is key to reaping the benefits of regular physical activity. Aim to make exercise a regular part of your daily routine, and find activities that you enjoy to stay motivated.

Nutrition and Healthy Eating for Older Adults

Proper nutrition is essential for maintaining health and well-being as we age. A balanced diet provides the nutrients needed to support physical health, cognitive function, and overall vitality. Healthy eating can help prevent chronic diseases, manage weight, and enhance the quality of life.

Nutritional Needs of Older Adults:

1. CALORIES:

As we age, our metabolism tends to slow down, and our caloric needs may decrease. However, it's important to ensure that the calories consumed come from nutrient-dense foods that provide essential vitamins and minerals.

2. Protein:

Protein is crucial for maintaining muscle mass and strength, supporting immune function, and promoting tissue repair. Older adults should aim to include high-quality protein sources in their diet, such as lean meats, poultry, fish, eggs, dairy products, legumes, nuts, and seeds.

3. Carbohydrates:

Carbohydrates provide energy and are an important source of fiber, which aids in digestion and helps prevent constipation. Choose complex carbohydrates such as whole grains, fruits, vegetables, and legumes, which provide sustained energy and important nutrients.

4. Fats:

Healthy fats are essential for brain health, hormone production, and overall well-being. Include sources of unsaturated fats, such as avocados, nuts, seeds, olive oil, and fatty fish, in your diet. Limit saturated fats and trans fats, which can increase the risk of heart disease.

5. Fiber:

Fiber is important for digestive health, blood sugar control, and heart health. Aim to include a variety of fiber-rich foods, such as fruits, vegetables, whole grains, legumes, nuts, and seeds, in your diet.

6. Vitamins and Minerals:

Older adults may need to pay special attention to certain vitamins and minerals, including:

- Calcium and Vitamin D: These nutrients are important for bone health. Include sources of calcium (dairy products, leafy greens, fortified foods) and vitamin D (fatty fish, fortified foods, sun exposure) in your diet.

- Vitamin B12: Absorption of vitamin B12 may decrease with age. Include sources of B12 (meat, fish, dairy products, fortified foods) or consider a supplement if recommended by your healthcare provider.

- Iron: Iron is essential for preventing anemia. Include sources of iron (lean meats, beans, fortified cereals) and vitamin C-rich foods (citrus fruits, bell peppers) to enhance absorption.

- Potassium: Potassium helps regulate blood pressure and supports heart health. Include sources of potassium (fruits, vegetables, dairy products) in your diet.

Healthy Eating Habits:

1. EAT A VARIETY OF Foods:

A varied diet ensures that you get a wide range of nutrients. Include a colorful array of fruits and vegetables, whole grains, lean proteins, and healthy fats in your meals.

2. Control Portion Sizes:

Pay attention to portion sizes to avoid overeating. Using smaller plates, measuring portions, and being mindful of serving sizes can help you manage your calorie intake.

3. Stay Hydrated:

Adequate hydration is important for overall health. Drink plenty of water throughout the day, and limit sugary beverages and excessive caffeine. Herbal teas and water-rich foods, such as fruits and vegetables, can also contribute to hydration.

4. Limit Added Sugars and Sodium:

Reduce your intake of added sugars and sodium, which can contribute to chronic health conditions such as diabetes and hypertension. Choose fresh, whole foods over processed and packaged items, and read nutrition labels to monitor your intake.

5. Plan Balanced Meals:

Aim to include a balance of macronutrients (carbohydrates, proteins, fats) and micronutrients (vitamins, minerals) in each meal. A well-balanced plate typically includes a source of lean protein, whole grains, and a variety of colorful vegetables and fruits.

6. Practice Mindful Eating:

Mindful eating involves paying attention to the sensory experiences of eating, such as the taste, texture, and aroma of food. Eating slowly and savoring each bite can enhance enjoyment and prevent overeating.

Meal Planning Tips:

1. CREATE A WEEKLY Meal Plan:

Plan your meals for the week to ensure you have a variety of nutritious options. A meal plan can help you make healthier choices and reduce the temptation to opt for convenience foods.

2. Prepare Meals in Advance:

Preparing meals in advance can save time and make it easier to stick to healthy eating habits. Batch cooking and freezing portions can provide quick and convenient meals throughout the week.

3. Include Snacks:

Healthy snacks can help maintain energy levels and prevent overeating at mealtimes. Choose nutrient-dense snacks such as fresh fruit, yogurt, nuts, seeds, and whole-grain crackers.

4. Incorporate Seasonal and Local Foods:

Seasonal and local foods are often fresher and more nutrient-dense. Visit farmers' markets and explore seasonal produce to add variety and flavor to your meals.

5. Make Eating a Social Activity:

Eating with others can enhance the enjoyment of meals and provide an opportunity for social interaction. Share meals with family and friends, and participate in community dining events.

Special Considerations for Older Adults:

1. APPETITE CHANGES:

Appetite may decrease with age due to changes in taste, smell, and digestive function. Focus on nutrient-dense foods and consider smaller, more frequent meals if needed.

2. Dental Health:

Dental issues, such as missing teeth or dentures, can affect the ability to chew certain foods. Choose softer foods and ensure that meals are easy to chew and swallow.

3. Digestive Health:

Digestive health can change with age, leading to issues such as constipation or acid reflux. Include fiber-rich foods, stay hydrated, and consider probiotics to support digestive health.

4. Medication Interactions:

Certain medications can interact with nutrients and affect absorption. Discuss any potential interactions with your healthcare provider and consider dietary adjustments as needed.

5. Food Safety:

Older adults may be more susceptible to foodborne illnesses. Practice food safety by properly storing, handling, and cooking food. Avoid raw or undercooked foods, and be mindful of expiration dates.

Sample Meal Plan for Older Adults:

BREAKFAST:

- Oatmeal topped with fresh berries, a sprinkle of nuts, and a drizzle of honey

- A glass of low-fat milk or a dairy alternative fortified with calcium and vitamin D

Mid-Morning Snack:

- A SMALL APPLE OR A handful of grapes

- A serving of Greek yogurt

Lunch:

- Grilled chicken salad with mixed greens, cherry tomatoes, cucumbers, and avocado, dressed with olive oil and lemon juice

- A slice of whole-grain bread

Afternoon Snack:

- A SMALL HANDFUL OF almonds or walnuts

- Carrot sticks with hummus

Dinner:

- Baked salmon with a side of quinoa

- Steamed broccoli and roasted sweet potatoes

- A glass of water or herbal tea

Evening Snack:

- A SMALL BOWL OF FRESH fruit salad

Preventive Healthcare and Regular Check-Ups

Preventive healthcare is crucial for maintaining health and well-being as we age. Regular check-ups, screenings, and preventive measures can help detect and manage health conditions early, reduce the risk of chronic diseases, and enhance the quality of life.

The Importance of Preventive Healthcare:

1. EARLY DETECTION of Health Issues:

Regular check-ups and screenings can help detect health issues early, when they are most treatable. Early detection can prevent the progression of diseases and improve health outcomes.

2. Management of Chronic Conditions:

Preventive healthcare helps manage chronic conditions such as diabetes, hypertension, and heart disease. Regular monitoring and appropriate interventions can prevent complications and improve quality of life.

3. Vaccinations and Immunizations:

Vaccinations and immunizations are essential for preventing infectious diseases. Older adults should stay up-to-date with recommended vaccines, such as the flu vaccine, pneumococcal vaccine, and shingles vaccine.

4. Health Education and Counseling:

Preventive healthcare includes health education and counseling on topics such as diet, exercise, smoking cessation, and mental health. Educating individuals about healthy lifestyle choices empowers them to take control of their health.

Recommended Preventive Screenings and Check-Ups:

1. ANNUAL PHYSICAL Exam:

An annual physical exam is a comprehensive check-up that assesses overall health and identifies any potential health issues. It includes a review of medical history, physical examination, and routine tests such as blood pressure measurement and blood tests.

2. Blood Pressure Screening:

Regular blood pressure screenings are important for detecting hypertension, a risk factor for heart disease and stroke. Blood pressure should be checked at least once a year.

3. Cholesterol Screening:

Cholesterol screenings help assess the risk of cardiovascular disease. A lipid panel measures total cholesterol, LDL cholesterol, HDL cholesterol, and triglycerides. Screening is typically recommended every 4-6 years, or more frequently if you have risk factors.

4. Blood Glucose Screening:

Blood glucose screenings detect diabetes and prediabetes. A fasting blood glucose test or an A1C test measures blood sugar levels. Screening is recommended every 3 years for adults over 45, or more frequently if you have risk factors.

5. Bone Density Test:

A bone density test, or DXA scan, measures bone strength and helps diagnose osteoporosis. It is typically recommended for women over 65 and men over 70, or earlier if you have risk factors.

6. Colorectal Cancer Screening:

Colorectal cancer screening detects precancerous polyps and early-stage colorectal cancer. Screening methods include colonoscopy, sigmoidoscopy, and stool tests. Screening is recommended for adults aged 50-75, or earlier if you have risk factors.

7. Breast Cancer Screening:

Mammograms detect early-stage breast cancer. Screening is recommended every 1-2 years for women aged 50-74, or earlier if you have risk factors.

8. Prostate Cancer Screening:

Prostate cancer screening includes a prostate-specific antigen (PSA) test and a digital rectal exam. Screening decisions should be made in consultation with your healthcare provider, based on individual risk factors.

9. Eye Exams:

Regular eye exams detect vision changes and eye conditions such as glaucoma, cataracts, and macular degeneration. Adults over 65 should have a comprehensive eye exam every 1-2 years.

10. Hearing Tests:

Hearing tests detect hearing loss and other auditory issues. Adults over 65 should have a hearing test every 3 years.

11. Dental Check-Ups:

Regular dental check-ups maintain oral health and detect dental issues. Dental exams and cleanings are typically recommended every 6 months.

Creating a Preventive Healthcare Plan:

1. SCHEDULE REGULAR Check-Ups:

Schedule regular check-ups with your primary care provider to monitor your overall health and address any concerns. Regular visits provide an opportunity to discuss your health goals and preventive measures.

2. Stay Up-to-Date with Screenings:

Keep track of recommended screenings and schedule them as needed. Create a health calendar to remind you of upcoming screenings and follow-up appointments.

3. Maintain Vaccinations:

Stay up-to-date with recommended vaccinations and immunizations. Discuss your vaccination needs with your healthcare provider and ensure you receive necessary vaccines.

4. Monitor Chronic Conditions:

If you have chronic conditions, work with your healthcare provider to manage them effectively. Regular monitoring, medication management, and lifestyle adjustments can prevent complications and improve quality of life.

5. Adopt a Healthy Lifestyle:

A healthy lifestyle supports preventive healthcare. Focus on regular physical activity, a balanced diet, adequate sleep, stress management, and avoiding harmful behaviors such as smoking and excessive alcohol consumption.

6. Engage in Health Education:

Stay informed about health and wellness topics. Attend health education workshops, read reliable health information, and engage in discussions with your healthcare provider.

Sample Preventive Healthcare Checklist:

MONTHLY:

- Self-breast exam (for women)

- Monitor blood pressure if you have hypertension

- Monitor blood glucose if you have diabetes

Every 3-6 Months:

- DENTAL CHECK-UP AND cleaning

- Hearing test if you have hearing concerns

Annually:

- Physical exam

- Blood pressure screening

- Cholesterol screening (as recommended)

- Blood glucose screening (as recommended)

- Eye exam

- Flu vaccine

- Skin check for unusual moles or changes

Every 1-2 Years:

- MAMMOGRAM (FOR WOMEN aged 50-74)

- Bone density test (as recommended)

Every 3 Years:

- COLORECTAL CANCER screening (as recommended)

- Prostate cancer screening (as recommended)

As Needed:

- VACCINATIONS (E.G., shingles, pneumococcal)

- Additional screenings based on risk factors

Case Studies: Embracing Preventive Healthcare

Case Study 1: Alice's Commitment to Preventive Health

ALICE, A 65-YEAR-OLD retiree, decided to prioritize preventive healthcare to maintain her health and well-being as she aged.

Alice's Strategies:

- REGULAR CHECK-UPS: Alice scheduled annual physical exams with her primary care provider to monitor her overall health and address any concerns.

- Screenings: Alice kept up-to-date with recommended screenings, including mammograms, bone density tests, and cholesterol checks.

- Vaccinations: Alice received her annual flu vaccine and ensured she was up-to-date with other vaccinations, including the shingles and pneumococcal vaccines.

- Healthy Lifestyle: Alice adopted a healthy lifestyle, focusing on regular exercise, a balanced diet, and stress management techniques such as yoga and meditation.

- Health Education: Alice attended health education workshops and stayed informed about wellness topics through reliable health resources.

Results:

Through her commitment to preventive healthcare, Alice maintained her health and well-being, reducing her risk of chronic diseases and detecting health issues early. Alice's experience highlighted the importance of proactive health management and regular check-ups.

Case Study 2: Bob's Journey to Wellness

BOB, A 70-YEAR-OLD retired engineer, embraced preventive healthcare to enhance his quality of life and manage his chronic conditions.

Bob's Strategies:

- CHRONIC CONDITION Management: Bob worked with his healthcare provider to manage his hypertension and diabetes. He monitored his blood pressure and blood glucose regularly and followed his prescribed medication regimen.

- Regular Screenings: Bob kept up-to-date with preventive screenings, including colonoscopies, eye exams, and hearing tests.

- Vaccinations: Bob received his recommended vaccinations, including the flu vaccine and the shingles vaccine.

- Healthy Diet: Bob adopted a balanced diet rich in fruits, vegetables, whole grains, and lean proteins. He also practiced portion control and stayed hydrated.

- Physical Activity: Bob engaged in regular physical activity, including daily walks, strength training, and tai chi for balance and flexibility.

- Stress Management: Bob practiced mindfulness meditation and engaged in hobbies such as gardening and woodworking to manage stress.

Results:

Bob's commitment to preventive healthcare and a healthy lifestyle helped him manage his chronic conditions effectively and maintain his overall well-being. Bob's journey demonstrated the impact of preventive measures on health and quality of life.

Conclusion

Physical health and wellness are essential components of aging well. By prioritizing regular physical activity, adopting a balanced diet, and embracing preventive healthcare, older adults can enhance their overall well-being, reduce the risk of chronic diseases, and enjoy a fulfilling and vibrant life.

In this chapter, we explored the importance of regular physical activity, nutrition and healthy eating for older adults, and the role of preventive healthcare and regular check-ups. By integrating these practices into your daily life, you can support your physical health, boost your energy levels, and maintain your independence as you age.

As you continue to explore the strategies for mind, body, and spirit outlined in this book, remember that taking care of your physical health is a crucial aspect of living your best life at any age. Embrace the journey of aging with a proactive and positive attitude, and prioritize your physical well-being to enjoy a long, healthy, and fulfilling life.

Chapter 4: Mental Health and Cognitive Wellness

Keeping the Mind Sharp with Mental Exercises

Mental exercises are crucial for maintaining cognitive health and keeping the mind sharp as we age. Engaging in activities that challenge the brain can enhance memory, improve problem-solving skills, and delay cognitive decline. Here, we explore various mental exercises and their benefits, along with practical ways to incorporate them into daily life.

The Importance of Mental Exercises:

1. IMPROVED MEMORY:

Regular mental exercises can enhance memory and recall abilities. Activities that challenge the brain, such as puzzles, memory games, and learning new skills, stimulate neural connections and support memory function.

2. Enhanced Problem-Solving Skills:

Mental exercises can improve problem-solving skills and cognitive flexibility. Engaging in tasks that require critical thinking and creativity helps keep the mind agile and responsive.

3. Delayed Cognitive Decline:

Studies have shown that mental exercises can delay the onset of cognitive decline and reduce the risk of dementia. Keeping the brain active and engaged promotes cognitive resilience and longevity.

4. Increased Focus and Concentration:

Mental exercises can improve focus and concentration by training the brain to stay attentive and process information effectively. This is particularly beneficial for tasks that require sustained mental effort.

Types of Mental Exercises:

1. PUZZLES AND BRAIN Teasers:

Puzzles and brain teasers are excellent for stimulating cognitive function. Crosswords, Sudoku, jigsaw puzzles, and logic puzzles challenge the brain and promote problem-solving skills.

2. Memory Games:

Memory games, such as matching pairs, recall exercises, and memory-based card games, help enhance memory and recall abilities. These games can be played alone or with others for added enjoyment.

3. Learning New Skills:

Learning new skills, such as playing a musical instrument, speaking a new language, or mastering a new craft, engages different areas of the brain and promotes cognitive flexibility. Continuous learning keeps the brain active and adaptable.

4. Reading and Writing:

Reading books, articles, and other written materials stimulates the brain and enhances comprehension and critical thinking skills. Writing, whether journaling, creative writing, or composing essays, promotes cognitive function and self-expression.

5. Educational Activities:

Participating in educational activities, such as taking courses, attending lectures, or engaging in workshops, supports lifelong learning and cognitive health. Online courses and community classes offer opportunities for intellectual engagement.

6. Social Engagement:

Social interactions and conversations stimulate cognitive function and promote mental well-being. Engaging in discussions, group activities, and social events provides mental stimulation and emotional support.

Incorporating Mental Exercises into Daily Life:

1. SET ASIDE TIME FOR Mental Activities:

Dedicate time each day to engage in mental exercises. Even short, daily sessions can have a significant impact on cognitive health. Schedule mental activities as part of your routine to ensure consistency.

2. Challenge Yourself:

Choose activities that challenge your brain and push you out of your comfort zone. The more complex and engaging the task, the greater the cognitive benefits. Gradually increase the difficulty of your chosen activities to keep your brain stimulated.

3. Mix and Match Activities:

Incorporate a variety of mental exercises to engage different areas of the brain. Mixing and matching activities, such as puzzles, reading, and social interactions, provides comprehensive cognitive stimulation.

4. Stay Curious and Open to Learning:

Cultivate a mindset of curiosity and openness to learning. Embrace opportunities to explore new subjects, hobbies, and skills. Lifelong learning keeps the brain active and engaged.

5. Combine Mental and Physical Activities:

Combine mental exercises with physical activities for a holistic approach to cognitive health. Activities like dancing, yoga, and tai chi engage both the mind and body, promoting overall well-being.

Managing Stress and Anxiety

Stress and anxiety are common challenges that can impact mental health and cognitive function, particularly as we age. Learning to manage stress and anxiety effectively is crucial for maintaining mental well-being and cognitive resilience.

The Impact of Stress and Anxiety:

1. COGNITIVE IMPAIRMENT:

Chronic stress and anxiety can impair cognitive function, affecting memory, concentration, and decision-making abilities. Elevated stress levels can lead to cognitive decline over time.

2. Physical Health:

Stress and anxiety can negatively impact physical health, contributing to conditions such as hypertension, heart disease, and weakened immune function. Managing stress is essential for overall health and well-being.

3. Emotional Well-Being:

Prolonged stress and anxiety can lead to emotional distress, including feelings of overwhelm, irritability, and depression. Addressing these emotions is vital for maintaining mental and emotional balance.

Strategies for Managing Stress and Anxiety:

1. Mindfulness and Meditation:

MINDFULNESS AND MEDITATION practices are effective tools for managing stress and anxiety. These practices promote relaxation, enhance self-awareness, and reduce the physiological effects of stress.

Steps to Practice Mindfulness and Meditation:

- FIND A QUIET SPACE: Choose a quiet and comfortable space where you can sit or lie down without distractions.

- Focus on Your Breath: Close your eyes and take slow, deep breaths. Focus on the sensation of your breath entering and leaving your body.

- Observe Without Judgment: Observe your thoughts and feelings without judgment. Allow them to come and go without getting attached to them.

- Practice Regularly: Set aside time each day for mindfulness and meditation. Even short sessions can have significant benefits for stress reduction.

2. Physical Activity:

REGULAR PHYSICAL ACTIVITY is a powerful stress reliever. Exercise releases endorphins, which are natural mood elevators, and helps reduce stress hormones such as cortisol.

Steps to Incorporate Physical Activity:

- CHOOSE ACTIVITIES You Enjoy: Engage in physical activities that you enjoy, such as walking, swimming, dancing, or yoga. Enjoyable activities are more likely to become regular habits.

- Stay Consistent: Aim for at least 150 minutes of moderate-intensity aerobic exercise per week. Consistency is key to reaping the stress-relieving benefits of physical activity.

- Combine Exercise with Nature: Exercising in nature, such as walking in a park or hiking, can enhance the stress-relieving effects. Nature provides a calming and rejuvenating environment.

3. Relaxation Techniques:

RELAXATION TECHNIQUES, such as deep breathing exercises, progressive muscle relaxation, and guided imagery, can help reduce stress and promote relaxation.

Steps to Practice Relaxation Techniques:

- DEEP BREATHING: PRACTICE deep breathing by inhaling slowly through your nose, holding your breath for a few seconds, and exhaling slowly through your mouth. Repeat several times.

- Progressive Muscle Relaxation: Tense and then relax each muscle group in your body, starting from your toes and working up to your head. This technique helps release physical tension.

- Guided Imagery: Visualize a peaceful and calming scene, such as a beach or a forest. Use your imagination to engage all your senses and create a vivid mental image.

4. Healthy Lifestyle Choices:

ADOPTING A HEALTHY lifestyle can help manage stress and anxiety. A balanced diet, adequate sleep, and avoiding harmful behaviors contribute to overall well-being.

Steps to Adopt Healthy Lifestyle Choices:

- BALANCED DIET: EAT a balanced diet rich in fruits, vegetables, whole grains, lean proteins, and healthy fats. Proper nutrition supports physical and mental health.

- Adequate Sleep: Aim for 7-9 hours of quality sleep each night. Establish a regular sleep schedule and create a relaxing bedtime routine to improve sleep quality.

- Avoid Harmful Behaviors: Limit or avoid alcohol, caffeine, and nicotine, which can exacerbate stress and anxiety. Avoid excessive screen time and prioritize activities that promote relaxation.

5. Social Support:

BUILDING AND MAINTAINING social connections provides emotional support and helps reduce feelings of stress and anxiety. Sharing your feelings with trusted friends and family members can provide relief and perspective.

Steps to Build and Maintain Social Support:

- STAY CONNECTED: MAKE an effort to stay connected with friends, family, and community. Regular communication, whether in person, over the phone, or through virtual means, strengthens relationships.

- Join Support Groups: Join support groups or social clubs that align with your interests. Participating in group activities provides opportunities for social interaction and emotional support.

- Seek Professional Help: If stress and anxiety become overwhelming, seek professional help from a therapist or counselor. Professional support can provide coping strategies and personalized guidance.

Strategies for Maintaining Cognitive Function

Maintaining cognitive function is essential for preserving mental sharpness and overall quality of life as we age. Cognitive wellness involves adopting habits and strategies that support brain health and prevent cognitive decline.

Key Strategies for Maintaining Cognitive Function:

1. Mental Stimulation:

ENGAGING IN MENTALLY stimulating activities keeps the brain active and promotes cognitive health. Lifelong learning, puzzles, games, and creative pursuits are effective ways to stimulate the mind.

Steps to Incorporate Mental Stimulation:

- PURSUE NEW INTERESTS: Explore new hobbies, skills, and subjects that interest you. Learning something new challenges the brain and enhances cognitive flexibility.

- Engage in Puzzles and Games: Regularly engage in puzzles, brain teasers, and games that require problem-solving and critical thinking. These activities stimulate different areas of the brain.

- Attend Educational Events: Participate in lectures, workshops, and courses that align with your interests. Educational events provide opportunities for intellectual engagement and social interaction.

2. Physical Activity:

PHYSICAL ACTIVITY SUPPORTS cognitive function by increasing blood flow to the brain and promoting the growth of new neural connections.

Exercise also reduces the risk of chronic conditions that can impact cognitive health.

Steps to Incorporate Physical Activity:

- CHOOSE ENJOYABLE ACTIVITIES: Engage in physical activities that you enjoy and can sustain over time. Walking, swimming, dancing, and yoga are excellent options.

- Include Aerobic and Strength Training: Combine aerobic exercises, which boost cardiovascular health, with strength training exercises that enhance muscle mass and bone density.

- Stay Consistent: Aim for at least 150 minutes of moderate-intensity exercise per week. Consistent physical activity supports overall health and cognitive function.

3. Healthy Diet:

A BALANCED DIET RICH in nutrients supports brain health and cognitive function. Certain foods have been shown to benefit brain health, including those rich in antioxidants, omega-3 fatty acids, and vitamins.

Steps to Adopt a Brain-Healthy Diet:

- EAT ANTIOXIDANT-RICH Foods: Include foods high in antioxidants, such as berries, leafy greens, nuts, and dark chocolate. Antioxidants protect brain cells from oxidative stress.

- Consume Omega-3 Fatty Acids: Incorporate sources of omega-3 fatty acids, such as fatty fish, flaxseeds, chia seeds, and walnuts. Omega-3s support brain structure and function.

- Prioritize Whole Foods: Focus on whole foods, such as fruits, vegetables, whole grains, lean proteins, and healthy fats. These foods provide essential nutrients for brain health.

4. Social Engagement:

SOCIAL INTERACTIONS stimulate cognitive function and support mental well-being. Building and maintaining relationships provides intellectual and emotional stimulation.

Steps to Enhance Social Engagement:

- STAY CONNECTED: MAINTAIN regular contact with family, friends, and community members. Social interactions provide mental stimulation and emotional support.

- Join Social Groups: Participate in social groups, clubs, or organizations that align with your interests. Group activities offer opportunities for meaningful interactions and intellectual engagement.

- Volunteer: Volunteering provides a sense of purpose and opportunities for social interaction. Engaging in community service enhances cognitive and emotional well-being.

5. Adequate Sleep:

QUALITY SLEEP IS ESSENTIAL for cognitive health. During sleep, the brain processes information, consolidates memories, and clears out toxins. Prioritizing good sleep hygiene supports cognitive function.

Steps to Improve Sleep Quality:

- ESTABLISH A SLEEP Routine: Create a regular sleep schedule by going to bed and waking up at the same time each day. Consistency helps regulate your sleep-wake cycle.

- Create a Relaxing Bedtime Routine: Develop a relaxing bedtime routine that signals to your body that it's time to wind down. This may include activities such as reading, meditating, or taking a warm bath.

- Optimize Your Sleep Environment: Ensure your sleep environment is conducive to rest by keeping your bedroom cool, dark, and quiet. Invest in a comfortable mattress and pillows.

6. Stress Management:

MANAGING STRESS IS crucial for maintaining cognitive function. Chronic stress can impair memory and cognitive abilities. Adopting stress-reducing practices supports brain health.

Steps to Manage Stress:

- PRACTICE MINDFULNESS and Meditation: Engage in mindfulness and meditation practices to reduce stress and promote relaxation. These practices enhance self-awareness and emotional regulation.

- Incorporate Relaxation Techniques: Use relaxation techniques such as deep breathing, progressive muscle relaxation, and guided imagery to manage stress and calm the mind.

- Stay Active: Physical activity is a natural stress reliever. Regular exercise reduces stress hormones and boosts mood-enhancing endorphins.

7. Avoid Harmful Behaviors:

CERTAIN BEHAVIORS, such as smoking and excessive alcohol consumption, can negatively impact cognitive health. Avoiding harmful behaviors supports overall brain health.

Steps to Avoid Harmful Behaviors:

- QUIT SMOKING: IF YOU smoke, seek support to quit. Smoking is associated with an increased risk of cognitive decline and dementia.

- Limit Alcohol Consumption: Limit alcohol intake to moderate levels. Excessive alcohol consumption can impair cognitive function and increase the risk of cognitive decline.

- Stay Informed: Educate yourself about the potential impact of harmful behaviors on cognitive health. Awareness can motivate positive changes.

8. Engage in Creative Activities:

CREATIVE ACTIVITIES, such as art, music, and writing, stimulate the brain and enhance cognitive function. These activities promote self-expression and mental engagement.

Steps to Engage in Creative Activities:

- EXPLORE ARTISTIC PURSUITS: Try your hand at painting, drawing, sculpting, or other forms of visual art. Artistic activities engage different areas of the brain and foster creativity.

- Play Music: Learn to play a musical instrument or sing. Music stimulates the brain, enhances memory, and promotes emotional well-being.

- Write Regularly: Engage in writing activities, such as journaling, creative writing, or composing poetry. Writing supports cognitive function and self-expression.

Case Studies: Maintaining Cognitive Function

Case Study 1: Susan's Journey to Cognitive Wellness

Susan, a 70-year-old retired teacher, decided to prioritize cognitive wellness by incorporating various strategies into her daily routine.

Susan's Strategies:

- MENTAL STIMULATION: Susan engaged in daily puzzles, such as crosswords and Sudoku, to challenge her brain. She also took up learning a new language through online courses.

- Physical Activity: Susan incorporated regular physical activity, including brisk walking and yoga, into her routine. She found that exercise boosted her energy levels and mental clarity.

- Healthy Diet: Susan adopted a brain-healthy diet rich in antioxidants, omega-3 fatty acids, and whole foods. She included berries, leafy greens, fatty fish, and nuts in her meals.

- Social Engagement: Susan joined a local book club and participated in community events. These activities provided intellectual stimulation and social connections.

- Mindfulness Meditation: Susan practiced mindfulness meditation daily to manage stress and promote relaxation. She found that meditation improved her focus and emotional well-being.

Results:

Through her commitment to cognitive wellness, Susan experienced enhanced cognitive function, improved memory, and better overall well-being. Susan's journey highlighted the benefits of a comprehensive approach to maintaining cognitive health.

Case Study 2: Tom's Path to Mental Sharpness

TOM, A 68-YEAR-OLD retired engineer, embraced strategies to keep his mind sharp and maintain cognitive function.

Tom's Strategies:

- LEARNING NEW SKILLS: Tom took up woodworking and enrolled in online courses to learn about different woodworking techniques. These activities challenged his problem-solving skills and creativity.

- Physical Activity: Tom engaged in regular physical activity, including swimming and strength training. He found that exercise improved his mood and cognitive function.

- Social Connections: Tom maintained regular contact with friends and family and participated in social clubs. Social interactions provided mental stimulation and emotional support.

- Healthy Lifestyle: Tom adopted a balanced diet, prioritized quality sleep, and avoided harmful behaviors such as excessive alcohol consumption. These lifestyle choices supported his overall health and cognitive function.

- Stress Management: Tom practiced relaxation techniques, such as deep breathing and guided imagery, to manage stress. These practices helped him stay calm and focused.

Results:

By prioritizing mental sharpness and cognitive wellness, Tom maintained his cognitive function and overall well-being. Tom's path demonstrated the impact of proactive strategies on cognitive health.

Conclusion

Mental health and cognitive wellness are essential components of aging well. By engaging in mental exercises, managing stress and anxiety, and adopting strategies to maintain cognitive function, older adults can enhance their mental sharpness, emotional well-being, and overall quality of life.

In this chapter, we explored the importance of keeping the mind sharp with mental exercises, effective strategies for managing stress and anxiety, and key approaches to maintaining cognitive function. By integrating these practices into your daily life, you can support your mental and cognitive health, build resilience, and enjoy a fulfilling and vibrant life as you age.

As you continue to explore the strategies for mind, body, and spirit outlined in this book, remember that taking care of your mental health is a crucial aspect of living your best life at any age. Embrace the journey of aging with a proactive and positive attitude, and prioritize your mental well-being to enjoy a long, healthy, and fulfilling life.

Chapter 5: Emotional Well-Being

Recognizing and Addressing Emotional Needs

Emotional well-being is a fundamental aspect of aging well. It involves understanding and addressing our emotional needs, building resilience to cope with life's changes, and nurturing relationships and social connections. Emotional health influences our overall quality of life, affecting how we feel about ourselves, how we interact with others, and how we navigate life's challenges.

Understanding Emotional Needs:

1. EMOTIONAL AWARENESS:

Emotional awareness is the ability to recognize and understand our own emotions. It involves being attuned to how we feel in different situations and understanding the underlying causes of those emotions. Emotional awareness is the first step in addressing our emotional needs.

2. Emotional Regulation:

Emotional regulation is the ability to manage and respond to our emotions in healthy ways. It involves strategies for coping with negative emotions, such as stress, anxiety, and sadness, and fostering positive emotions, such as joy, gratitude, and contentment.

3. Emotional Expression:

Emotional expression is the ability to communicate our emotions effectively. This includes expressing our feelings to others and finding healthy outlets for emotional release, such as writing, art, or physical activity.

4. Emotional Support:

Emotional support involves seeking and receiving support from others. This can include talking to friends and family members, seeking professional help, or participating in support groups. Emotional support provides a sense of connection and helps us navigate difficult times.

Recognizing Emotional Needs:

1. Self-Reflection:

SELF-REFLECTION IS a powerful tool for recognizing our emotional needs. Taking time to reflect on our feelings, thoughts, and experiences helps us understand what we need to feel emotionally balanced and fulfilled.

Steps to Practice Self-Reflection:

- JOURNALING: KEEP A journal to record your thoughts, feelings, and experiences. Writing about your emotions can help you gain insight into your emotional needs and patterns.

- Mindfulness: Practice mindfulness by paying attention to your emotions in the present moment. Notice how you feel without judgment and observe the triggers and patterns of your emotions.

- Quiet Time: Set aside quiet time for self-reflection. This could be during a walk, meditation, or simply sitting in a peaceful environment. Use this time to explore your emotions and understand what you need to feel emotionally well.

2. Identifying Emotional Triggers:

IDENTIFYING EMOTIONAL triggers involves recognizing the situations, people, or events that evoke strong emotional reactions. Understanding our triggers helps us anticipate and manage our emotions more effectively.

Steps to Identify Emotional Triggers:

- OBSERVE REACTIONS: Pay attention to your emotional reactions in different situations. Notice when you feel particularly stressed, anxious, happy, or sad.

- Analyze Patterns: Look for patterns in your emotional reactions. Are there specific situations or people that consistently trigger certain emotions?

- Reflect on Causes: Reflect on the underlying causes of your emotional triggers. What is it about the situation or person that evokes a strong emotional response?

3. Understanding Emotional Needs:

UNDERSTANDING EMOTIONAL needs involves recognizing what we require to feel emotionally balanced and fulfilled. This can include needs for love, connection, security, recognition, and self-expression.

Steps to Understand Emotional Needs:

- REFLECT ON PAST EXPERIENCES: Think about past experiences when you felt emotionally fulfilled or distressed. What needs were being met or unmet in those situations?

- Identify Core Needs: Identify your core emotional needs. These could include needs for connection, autonomy, competence, or self-acceptance.

- Assess Current Needs: Assess your current emotional needs. Are there areas in your life where your emotional needs are not being met? What changes can you make to address these needs?

Addressing Emotional Needs:

1. Practicing Self-Care:

SELF-CARE INVOLVES taking intentional actions to care for our emotional, mental, and physical well-being. Practicing self-care helps us address our emotional needs and maintain emotional balance.

Steps to Practice Self-Care:

- SET BOUNDARIES: SET healthy boundaries to protect your emotional well-being. This could involve saying no to activities or people that drain your energy or stress you out.

- Engage in Activities You Enjoy: Make time for activities that bring you joy and fulfillment. This could include hobbies, exercise, creative pursuits, or spending time with loved ones.

- Prioritize Rest: Ensure you get enough rest and relaxation. Prioritize sleep, take breaks when needed, and practice relaxation techniques to recharge your energy.

2. Seeking Emotional Support:

SEEKING EMOTIONAL SUPPORT involves reaching out to others for help, understanding, and connection. Emotional support from friends, family, or professionals provides a sense of belonging and helps us navigate difficult emotions.

Steps to Seek Emotional Support:

- TALK TO LOVED ONES: Share your feelings and experiences with trusted friends or family members. Talking about your emotions can provide relief and help you gain perspective.

- Join Support Groups: Join support groups or online communities where you can connect with others who share similar experiences. Support groups provide a safe space to share and receive support.

- Seek Professional Help: If you're struggling with intense emotions or mental health challenges, consider seeking help from a therapist or counselor. Professional support can provide strategies for managing emotions and improving emotional well-being.

3. Developing Healthy Coping Strategies:

HEALTHY COPING STRATEGIES help us manage difficult emotions and navigate life's challenges. Developing effective coping mechanisms enhances our emotional resilience and well-being.

Steps to Develop Healthy Coping Strategies:

- PRACTICE MINDFULNESS and Relaxation: Engage in mindfulness practices, such as meditation, deep breathing, or progressive muscle relaxation, to calm your mind and body.

- Engage in Physical Activity: Physical activity releases endorphins and helps reduce stress. Find activities you enjoy, such as walking, dancing, or yoga, and make them a regular part of your routine.

- Express Emotions Creatively: Find creative outlets for expressing your emotions, such as writing, drawing, painting, or playing music. Creative expression provides a healthy release for emotions.

4. Building Resilience and Coping with Change:

RESILIENCE IS THE ABILITY to adapt and thrive in the face of adversity and change. Building resilience involves developing skills and strategies to cope with challenges, bounce back from setbacks, and maintain emotional well-being.

The Importance of Resilience:

1. ADAPTATION TO CHANGE:

Resilience helps us adapt to life's changes and transitions. Whether it's retirement, loss, or health challenges, resilience enables us to navigate change with flexibility and strength.

2. Emotional Stability:

Resilience contributes to emotional stability by helping us manage stress, anxiety, and negative emotions. It allows us to maintain a positive outlook and emotional balance, even in difficult times.

3. Improved Problem-Solving:

Resilient individuals are better equipped to solve problems and make decisions under pressure. Resilience enhances our ability to think clearly and act effectively in challenging situations.

Strategies for Building Resilience:

1. Developing a Growth Mindset:

A GROWTH MINDSET IS the belief that we can learn, grow, and improve through effort and perseverance. Developing a growth mindset enhances resilience by fostering a positive attitude toward challenges and setbacks.

Steps to Develop a Growth Mindset:

- EMBRACE CHALLENGES: View challenges as opportunities for growth and learning. Approach difficulties with curiosity and a willingness to learn from them.

- Learn from Setbacks: Reflect on setbacks and identify lessons learned. Use these insights to improve and move forward.

- Celebrate Effort and Progress: Acknowledge and celebrate your efforts and progress, regardless of the outcome. Recognize that growth and improvement come from persistence and hard work.

2. Strengthening Problem-Solving Skills:

EFFECTIVE PROBLEM-SOLVING skills enhance resilience by helping us navigate challenges and find solutions. Strengthening these skills involves developing strategies for analyzing and addressing problems.

Steps to Strengthen Problem-Solving Skills:

- IDENTIFY THE PROBLEM: Clearly define the problem or challenge you're facing. Break it down into manageable parts to better understand it.

- Brainstorm Solutions: Generate a list of possible solutions or approaches. Consider different perspectives and think creatively about potential options.

- Evaluate Options: Assess the pros and cons of each solution. Consider the potential outcomes and feasibility of each option.

- Take Action: Choose the best solution and take action. Monitor the results and adjust your approach as needed.

3. Building a Support Network:

A STRONG SUPPORT NETWORK provides emotional and practical support, enhancing our resilience. Building and maintaining relationships with supportive individuals helps us navigate challenges and feel connected.

Steps to Build a Support Network:

- NURTURE EXISTING RELATIONSHIPS: Strengthen your connections with friends, family, and colleagues. Spend quality time with loved ones and communicate regularly.

- Seek New Connections: Join social groups, clubs, or organizations that align with your interests. Participating in group activities provides opportunities to meet new people and build relationships.

- Offer Support to Others: Be a source of support for others. Offering help and encouragement fosters reciprocal relationships and strengthens your support network.

4. Practicing Self-Compassion:

SELF-COMPASSION INVOLVES treating ourselves with kindness, understanding, and acceptance, especially during difficult times. Practicing self-compassion enhances resilience by promoting emotional well-being and reducing self-criticism.

Steps to Practice Self-Compassion:

- BE KIND TO YOURSELF: Treat yourself with the same kindness and understanding that you would offer to a friend. Avoid harsh self-criticism and negative self-talk.

- Acknowledge Your Feelings: Recognize and validate your feelings, whether they are positive or negative. Allow yourself to experience and process your emotions without judgment.

- Practice Mindfulness: Engage in mindfulness practices to stay present and aware of your experiences. Mindfulness enhances self-compassion by promoting acceptance and non-judgmental awareness.

The Role of Relationships and Social Connections

Relationships and social connections are vital for emotional well-being. They provide emotional support, reduce feelings of loneliness, and enhance our sense of belonging. Nurturing relationships and building social connections contribute to a fulfilling and enriched life.

The Importance of Relationships:

1. EMOTIONAL SUPPORT:

Relationships provide emotional support, helping us navigate difficult emotions and challenges. Sharing our feelings and experiences with others offers comfort, understanding, and encouragement.

2. Sense of Belonging:

Social connections create a sense of belonging and community. Feeling connected to others enhances our self-worth and contributes to overall well-being.

3. Enhanced Quality of Life:

Strong relationships and social connections enhance our quality of life by providing opportunities for joy, companionship, and shared experiences. Engaging in social activities and spending time with loved ones enriches our lives.

Building and Nurturing Relationships:

1. COMMUNICATION:

Effective communication is the foundation of healthy relationships. Open, honest, and respectful communication fosters understanding and strengthens connections.

Steps to Improve Communication:

- ACTIVE LISTENING: Practice active listening by fully focusing on the speaker, avoiding interruptions, and responding thoughtfully. Active listening demonstrates empathy and understanding.

- Expressing Emotions: Share your feelings and experiences openly and honestly. Use "I" statements to express your emotions without blaming or criticizing others.

- Respectful Dialogue: Engage in respectful dialogue by valuing different perspectives and avoiding judgment. Approach conversations with curiosity and a willingness to understand.

2. Quality Time:

SPENDING QUALITY TIME with loved ones strengthens relationships and creates meaningful connections. Prioritize time for shared activities and experiences.

Steps to Spend Quality Time:

- SCHEDULE REGULAR ACTIVITIES: Plan regular activities with friends and family, such as meals, outings, or hobbies. Consistent time together fosters connection and enjoyment.

- Engage in Shared Interests: Participate in activities that you and your loved ones enjoy. Shared interests provide opportunities for bonding and positive experiences.

- Be Present: Be fully present during your time together. Avoid distractions, such as phones or work, and focus on enjoying each other's company.

3. Empathy and Compassion:

EMPATHY AND COMPASSION are essential for building strong relationships. Understanding and caring for others' feelings and experiences fosters connection and trust.

Steps to Practice Empathy and Compassion:

- PUT YOURSELF IN THEIR Shoes: Try to understand the perspective and feelings of others. Consider how you would feel in their situation.

- Offer Support: Provide emotional and practical support to those in need. Offering a listening ear, a kind word, or assistance demonstrates compassion and care.

- Practice Non-Judgment: Approach others with non-judgmental acceptance. Avoid criticizing or judging their experiences and emotions.

4. Resolving Conflicts:

CONFLICTS ARE A NATURAL part of relationships, but resolving them effectively is crucial for maintaining healthy connections. Addressing conflicts with empathy and respect strengthens relationships.

Steps to Resolve Conflicts:

- ADDRESS ISSUES PROMPTLY: Address conflicts and misunderstandings as soon as they arise. Avoiding issues can lead to resentment and strained relationships.

- Stay Calm: Approach conflicts with a calm and composed demeanor. Staying calm helps facilitate productive and respectful dialogue.

- Seek Compromise: Look for solutions that meet the needs of all parties involved. Compromise and collaboration foster mutual understanding and resolution.

5. Building New Connections:

BUILDING NEW CONNECTIONS expands our social network and provides opportunities for new friendships and experiences. Embrace opportunities to meet new people and build relationships.

Steps to Build New Connections:

- JOIN SOCIAL GROUPS: Join social groups, clubs, or organizations that align with your interests. Participating in group activities provides opportunities to meet new people.

- Attend Community Events: Attend community events, such as festivals, workshops, or social gatherings. Community events offer a chance to connect with others and engage in shared activities.

- Be Open and Approachable: Approach new interactions with an open and friendly attitude. Be approachable and show genuine interest in getting to know others.

Case Studies: Nurturing Emotional Well-Being

Case Study 1: Lisa's Journey to Emotional Balance

Lisa, a 68-year-old retired nurse, recognized the importance of addressing her emotional needs and building resilience to cope with life's changes.

Lisa's Strategies:

- SELF-REFLECTION: LISA practiced journaling and mindfulness to gain insight into her emotions and identify her emotional needs. This self-reflection helped her understand what she needed to feel emotionally balanced.

- Self-Care: Lisa engaged in self-care activities, such as gardening, reading, and yoga. These activities brought her joy and helped her maintain emotional balance.

- Seeking Support: Lisa sought emotional support from her friends and family. She joined a local support group where she could share her experiences and receive understanding and encouragement.

- Building Resilience: Lisa developed a growth mindset and practiced self-compassion. She embraced challenges as opportunities for growth and treated herself with kindness and understanding.

Results:

Through her commitment to emotional well-being, Lisa experienced enhanced emotional balance, resilience, and overall well-being. Lisa's journey highlighted the importance of recognizing and addressing emotional needs and building resilience.

Case Study 2: Mark's Path to Social Connection

MARK, A 72-YEAR-OLD retired engineer, recognized the value of relationships and social connections for his emotional well-being.

Mark's Strategies:

- COMMUNICATION: MARK improved his communication skills by practicing active listening and expressing his emotions openly. This strengthened his relationships with friends and family.

- Quality Time: Mark prioritized spending quality time with his loved ones. He planned regular activities, such as family dinners and weekend outings, to enjoy shared experiences.

- Empathy and Compassion: Mark practiced empathy and compassion in his interactions. He made an effort to understand and support others' feelings and experiences.

- Building New Connections: Mark joined a local woodworking club and attended community events. These activities provided opportunities to meet new people and build friendships.

Results:

By nurturing his relationships and building social connections, Mark experienced enhanced emotional well-being, a sense of belonging, and a richer social life. Mark's path demonstrated the impact of relationships and social connections on emotional health.

Conclusion

Emotional well-being is a vital aspect of aging well. By recognizing and addressing our emotional needs, building resilience to cope with change, and nurturing relationships and social connections, we can enhance our overall quality of life and enjoy a fulfilling and enriched experience as we age.

In this chapter, we explored the importance of recognizing and addressing emotional needs, strategies for building resilience and coping with change, and the role of relationships and social connections in emotional well-being. By integrating these practices into your daily life, you can support your emotional health, build resilience, and cultivate meaningful relationships.

As you continue to explore the strategies for mind, body, and spirit outlined in this book, remember that taking care of your emotional well-being is a crucial aspect of living your best life at any age. Embrace the journey of aging with a proactive and positive attitude, and prioritize your emotional health to enjoy a long, healthy, and fulfilling life.

Chapter 6: Spiritual Growth and Fulfillment

Exploring Spirituality in the Later Stages of Life

As we age, the quest for spiritual growth and fulfillment often becomes more pronounced. The later stages of life present an opportunity for deeper reflection, self-discovery, and connection with something greater than ourselves. Spirituality can provide a sense of purpose, inner peace, and resilience, enhancing our overall well-being.

Understanding Spirituality:

1. DEFINITION OF SPIRITUALITY:

Spirituality is a broad and multifaceted concept that encompasses the search for meaning, purpose, and connection. It can involve religious beliefs and practices, but it also includes personal experiences, values, and relationships that give life deeper significance.

2. Individualized Nature:

Spirituality is highly individualized and can vary greatly from person to person. It is shaped by personal beliefs, cultural background, life experiences, and individual preferences. There is no single path to spirituality; it is a unique and personal journey.

3. Spiritual Growth:

Spiritual growth involves the ongoing process of exploring, understanding, and nurturing our spiritual beliefs and practices. It is about deepening our connection with ourselves, others, and the world around us, as well as finding meaning and fulfillment in our lives.

Exploring Spirituality in Later Life:

1. Reflecting on Life Experiences:

THE LATER STAGES OF life offer an opportunity to reflect on past experiences and the lessons they have taught us. This reflection can provide valuable insights into our values, beliefs, and what truly matters to us.

Steps to Reflect on Life Experiences:

- JOURNALING: KEEP A journal to document your life experiences, thoughts, and reflections. Writing about your journey can help you gain clarity and understanding.

- Life Review: Conduct a life review by looking back on significant events, achievements, and challenges. Consider how these experiences have shaped your beliefs and values.

- Storytelling: Share your life story with others, whether through writing, speaking, or creative expression. Storytelling can be a powerful way to process and honor your experiences.

2. Exploring New Spiritual Practices:

AGING PROVIDES AN OPPORTUNITY to explore new spiritual practices and traditions. Trying different practices can help you discover what resonates with you and enhances your sense of spiritual fulfillment.

Steps to Explore New Spiritual Practices:

- ATTEND SERVICES: ATTEND religious or spiritual services, ceremonies, or gatherings to experience different traditions and practices.

- Read Spiritual Literature: Read books, articles, and scriptures from various spiritual traditions to broaden your understanding and perspective.

- Engage in Workshops: Participate in workshops, retreats, or classes that focus on spiritual growth and development.

3. Deepening Existing Practices:

FOR THOSE WITH ESTABLISHED spiritual practices, the later stages of life can be a time to deepen and enrich these practices. This can involve dedicating more time to meditation, prayer, or other spiritual activities.

Steps to Deepen Existing Practices:

- SET INTENTIONS: SET clear intentions for your spiritual practice. Reflect on what you hope to achieve or experience through your spiritual activities.

- Create a Sacred Space: Designate a space in your home for spiritual practice. This space can serve as a sanctuary for meditation, prayer, or reflection.

- Practice Regularly: Dedicate regular time to your spiritual practices. Consistency helps deepen your connection and enhances the benefits of your practice.

4. Connecting with Nature:

NATURE CAN BE A POWERFUL source of spiritual inspiration and connection. Spending time in nature allows us to experience the beauty, wonder, and interconnectedness of life.

Steps to Connect with Nature:

- SPEND TIME OUTDOORS: Make a habit of spending time outdoors, whether it's walking in the park, hiking in the woods, or simply sitting in a garden. Nature provides a calming and rejuvenating environment.

- Observe and Appreciate: Take time to observe and appreciate the natural world around you. Notice the details, such as the colors, sounds, and scents of nature.

- Engage in Eco-Spiritual Practices: Participate in eco-spiritual practices, such as gardening, nature meditation, or environmental stewardship. These activities foster a sense of connection and responsibility to the Earth.

Practices for Spiritual Well-Being

Spiritual well-being involves nurturing our spiritual selves through practices that enhance our connection, purpose, and inner peace. These practices can take many forms, from meditation and prayer to creative expression and acts of service.

Key Practices for Spiritual Well-Being:

1. MEDITATION:

Meditation is a practice that involves focusing the mind and achieving a state of mental clarity and relaxation. It can help deepen our spiritual connection, reduce stress, and promote inner peace.

Steps to Practice Meditation:

- FIND A QUIET SPACE: Choose a quiet and comfortable space where you can meditate without distractions.

- Focus on Your Breath: Sit or lie down comfortably and focus on your breath. Breathe slowly and deeply, paying attention to the sensation of your breath entering and leaving your body.

- Observe Your Thoughts: Allow your thoughts to come and go without judgment. If your mind wanders, gently bring your focus back to your breath.

- Set a Regular Time: Practice meditation regularly, even if it's just for a few minutes each day. Consistency enhances the benefits of meditation.

2. Prayer:

Prayer is a practice of communicating with a higher power or the divine. It can provide comfort, guidance, and a sense of connection to something greater than ourselves.

Steps to Practice Prayer:

- SET AN INTENTION: Set an intention for your prayer. This could be expressing gratitude, seeking guidance, or offering support for others.

- Find a Comfortable Position: Find a comfortable position for prayer, whether sitting, standing, or kneeling.

- Speak or Think: Speak your prayer out loud or think it silently. Use your own words or recite prayers from your spiritual tradition.

- Reflect and Listen: After your prayer, take a moment to reflect and listen. Be open to any insights or feelings that may arise.

3. Gratitude Practices:

GRATITUDE PRACTICES involve recognizing and appreciating the positive aspects of our lives. They can enhance our sense of fulfillment and connection.

Steps to Practice Gratitude:

- KEEP A GRATITUDE JOURNAL: Write down three to five things you are grateful for each day. Reflecting on positive experiences fosters a sense of appreciation.

- Express Gratitude to Others: Take time to express gratitude to the people in your life. This could be through thank-you notes, verbal acknowledgments, or acts of kindness.

- Practice Mindful Gratitude: Throughout the day, take moments to pause and appreciate the beauty and goodness around you. Mindful gratitude enhances your awareness of positive experiences.

4. Creative Expression:

CREATIVE EXPRESSION, such as art, music, writing, or dance, can be a powerful way to connect with our inner selves and express our spirituality.

Steps to Practice Creative Expression:

- CHOOSE A MEDIUM: CHOOSE a creative medium that resonates with you, whether it's painting, playing an instrument, writing poetry, or dancing.

- Create Regularly: Make time for creative expression regularly. It doesn't have to be perfect; the act of creating is what matters.

- Express Your Emotions: Use your chosen medium to express your emotions, thoughts, and spiritual experiences. Creative expression provides a healthy outlet for self-exploration.

5. Acts of Service:

ACTS OF SERVICE INVOLVE helping others and contributing to the well-being of our community. Service can provide a sense of purpose and connection.

Steps to Practice Acts of Service:

- IDENTIFY OPPORTUNITIES: Look for opportunities to serve others in your community, such as volunteering at a local organization, helping a neighbor, or participating in community projects.

- Offer Your Skills: Offer your skills and talents to benefit others. Whether it's teaching, cooking, or providing companionship, your contributions make a difference.

- Reflect on Your Impact: Reflect on the impact of your service. Recognize the positive changes you are helping to create and the sense of fulfillment it brings.

6. Mindfulness and Presence:

MINDFULNESS INVOLVES being fully present in the moment and cultivating awareness of our thoughts, feelings, and surroundings. It enhances our connection to ourselves and the world around us.

Steps to Practice Mindfulness:

- ENGAGE IN MINDFUL Activities: Engage in activities mindfully, such as eating, walking, or listening. Focus on the sensations and experiences of the present moment.

- Practice Mindful Breathing: Practice mindful breathing by taking slow, deep breaths and paying attention to the sensation of your breath. This can be done anywhere and anytime.

- Observe Without Judgment: Observe your thoughts and feelings without judgment. Allow them to come and go, accepting them as part of your experience.

Finding Purpose and Meaning in Aging

Finding purpose and meaning in aging involves recognizing the unique opportunities and contributions that come with this stage of life. It is about embracing the wisdom and experience we have gained and using them to enrich our lives and the lives of others.

The Importance of Purpose and Meaning:

1. ENHANCED WELL-BEING:

Having a sense of purpose and meaning enhances our overall well-being. It provides motivation, direction, and a reason to get up in the morning.

2. Resilience and Adaptability:

Purpose and meaning enhance our resilience and ability to adapt to life's changes. They provide a sense of stability and continuity, even in the face of challenges.

3. Connection and Fulfillment:

Purpose and meaning foster a sense of connection to ourselves, others, and the world around us. They contribute to a deep sense of fulfillment and satisfaction.

Steps to Find Purpose and Meaning in Aging:

1. Reflect on Your Values and Passions:

REFLECTING ON YOUR values and passions helps you identify what is truly important to you and what brings you joy and fulfillment.

Steps to Reflect on Values and Passions:

- IDENTIFY CORE VALUES: Identify your core values by reflecting on what matters most to you. These could include family, community, creativity, learning, or helping others.

- Explore Passions: Explore your passions by considering the activities and interests that bring you joy and excitement. These could be hobbies, talents, or causes you care about.

- Align with Your Actions: Align your actions and choices with your values and passions. Engaging in activities that reflect your values and passions enhances your sense of purpose.

2. Set Meaningful Goals:

SETTING MEANINGFUL goals provides direction and motivation. Goals give us something to strive for and a sense of accomplishment when achieved.

Steps to Set Meaningful Goals:

- IDENTIFY YOUR ASPIRATIONS: Identify your aspirations by considering what you hope to achieve or experience. These could be personal, professional, or spiritual goals.

- Set Specific and Realistic Goals: Set specific and realistic goals that align with your values and passions. Break them down into manageable steps and create a plan to achieve them.

- Celebrate Progress: Celebrate your progress and achievements along the way. Recognize the effort and dedication you put into reaching your goals.

3. Engage in Lifelong Learning:

LIFELONG LEARNING INVOLVES continually seeking new knowledge, skills, and experiences. It keeps the mind active, fosters curiosity, and enhances our sense of purpose.

Steps to Engage in Lifelong Learning:

- PURSUE NEW INTERESTS: Explore new subjects, hobbies, and activities that interest you. Take classes, read books, or participate in workshops to learn something new.

- Stay Curious: Cultivate a mindset of curiosity and openness to new experiences. Approach each day with a willingness to learn and grow.

- Share Your Knowledge: Share your knowledge and experiences with others. Teaching, mentoring, or writing about your expertise provides a sense of purpose and contributes to the community.

4. Contribute to the Community:

CONTRIBUTING TO THE community through acts of service and involvement provides a sense of connection and purpose. It allows us to make a positive impact and feel valued.

Steps to Contribute to the Community:

- VOLUNTEER: VOLUNTEER your time and skills to local organizations, charities, or community projects. Volunteering provides opportunities to help others and build connections.

- Join Community Groups: Join community groups, clubs, or organizations that align with your interests and values. Participating in group activities fosters a sense of belonging and purpose.

- Advocate for Causes: Advocate for causes you care about by raising awareness, supporting initiatives, or participating in advocacy efforts. Your voice and actions can make a difference.

5. Embrace Life Transitions:

EMBRACING LIFE TRANSITIONS, such as retirement, empty nesting, or health changes, involves finding new opportunities for growth and fulfillment. It is about adapting to change with resilience and optimism.

Steps to Embrace Life Transitions:

- ACKNOWLEDGE CHANGES: Acknowledge and accept the changes that come with aging. Recognize that transitions are a natural part of life and offer opportunities for growth.

- Explore New Opportunities: Explore new opportunities that align with your values and interests. Consider how you can use your skills and experiences in new ways.

- Stay Positive: Maintain a positive attitude and focus on the possibilities and opportunities that lie ahead. Embrace change as an opportunity for renewal and growth.

6. Cultivate Relationships:

BUILDING AND NURTURING relationships with family, friends, and community members enhances our sense of purpose and connection. Relationships provide support, joy, and a sense of belonging.

Steps to Cultivate Relationships:

- STAY CONNECTED: MAINTAIN regular contact with family and friends. Schedule regular gatherings, phone calls, or virtual meetings to stay connected.

- Build New Connections: Build new connections by joining social groups, clubs, or organizations. Participating in group activities provides opportunities to meet new people.

- Foster Deep Connections: Foster deep and meaningful connections by engaging in open and honest communication. Share your thoughts, feelings, and experiences with others.

Case Studies: Finding Purpose and Meaning in Aging

Case Study 1: Jane's Journey to Spiritual Fulfillment

Jane, a 72-year-old retired teacher, found purpose and meaning in her later years by exploring new spiritual practices and contributing to her community.

Jane's Strategies:

- EXPLORING NEW PRACTICES: Jane explored new spiritual practices, such as meditation and mindfulness. She attended workshops and read books on spirituality to deepen her understanding.

- Acts of Service: Jane volunteered at a local community center, teaching reading and writing to children. Her contributions provided a sense of fulfillment and connection.

- Lifelong Learning: Jane pursued her passion for art by taking painting classes. Creative expression became a spiritual practice that brought her joy and inner peace.

- Connecting with Nature: Jane spent time in nature, walking in the park and gardening. Nature provided a sense of connection and tranquility.

Results:

Through her commitment to spiritual growth and community involvement, Jane experienced a deep sense of purpose and fulfillment. Jane's journey highlighted the transformative power of exploring spirituality and contributing to the well-being of others.

Case Study 2: Tom's Path to Purpose in Retirement

TOM, A 70-YEAR-OLD retired engineer, found purpose and meaning in retirement by engaging in lifelong learning and building relationships.

Tom's Strategies:

- LIFELONG LEARNING: Tom took up woodworking and joined a local woodworking club. Learning new skills and creating projects provided a sense of accomplishment and purpose.

- Building Relationships: Tom built relationships with fellow club members and participated in community events. These connections provided social support and a sense of belonging.

- Volunteering: Tom volunteered at a local nonprofit organization, using his engineering skills to help with maintenance projects. His contributions made a positive impact on the community.

- Reflecting on Values: Tom reflected on his values and passions, identifying what brought him joy and fulfillment. He aligned his activities with his core values.

Results:

By engaging in lifelong learning, building relationships, and contributing to the community, Tom found a renewed sense of purpose and meaning in retirement. Tom's path demonstrated the importance of staying active and connected in later life.

Conclusion

Spiritual growth and fulfillment are essential components of aging well. By exploring spirituality, engaging in practices for spiritual well-being, and finding purpose and meaning in aging, we can enhance our overall quality of life and enjoy a fulfilling and enriched experience in the later stages of life.

In this chapter, we explored the importance of spirituality in later life, key practices for spiritual well-being, and strategies for finding purpose and meaning. By integrating these practices into your daily life, you can support your spiritual health, build resilience, and cultivate a deep sense of fulfillment.

As you continue to explore the strategies for mind, body, and spirit outlined in this book, remember that spiritual growth and fulfillment are crucial aspects of living your best life at any age. Embrace the journey of aging with a proactive and positive attitude, and prioritize your spiritual well-being to enjoy a long, healthy, and fulfilling life.

Chapter 7: Financial Security and Planning

Importance of Financial Planning for Retirement

Financial security in retirement is a key component of overall well-being and peace of mind. Effective financial planning ensures that you have sufficient resources to maintain your lifestyle, cover healthcare costs, and enjoy your golden years without financial stress. This chapter will explore the importance of financial planning for retirement, strategies for managing finances and budgeting, and essential legal considerations such as wills, trusts, and healthcare directives.

Understanding the Importance of Financial Planning:

1. ENSURING FINANCIAL Stability:

Financial planning helps ensure that you have the necessary funds to support yourself throughout retirement. By planning ahead, you can avoid financial difficulties and maintain your desired standard of living.

2. Covering Healthcare Costs:

Healthcare expenses tend to increase with age. Financial planning allows you to budget for medical expenses, including routine care, medications, and potential long-term care needs.

3. Achieving Financial Goals:

Effective financial planning helps you achieve your financial goals, whether it's traveling, pursuing hobbies, or supporting family members. Setting clear goals and creating a plan to achieve them enhances your financial security.

4. Reducing Stress and Anxiety:

Financial uncertainty can lead to stress and anxiety. Having a well-thought-out financial plan provides peace of mind and allows you to enjoy your retirement without worrying about money.

Steps to Effective Financial Planning for Retirement:

1. Assessing Your Financial Situation:

THE FIRST STEP IN FINANCIAL planning is to assess your current financial situation. This involves evaluating your income, expenses, savings, and investments to understand your financial health.

Steps to Assess Your Financial Situation:

- TRACK INCOME AND EXPENSES: Keep a detailed record of your income and expenses. This helps you understand where your money is going and identify areas for potential savings.

- Evaluate Savings and Investments: Review your savings accounts, retirement funds, and investment portfolios. Assess the performance of your investments and determine if they align with your retirement goals.

- Calculate Net Worth: Calculate your net worth by subtracting your liabilities (debts) from your assets (savings, investments, property). Your net worth provides a snapshot of your financial health.

2. Setting Retirement Goals:

SETTING CLEAR RETIREMENT goals helps guide your financial planning efforts. Consider your desired lifestyle, retirement age, and any specific goals you want to achieve during retirement.

Steps to Set Retirement Goals:

- DEFINE YOUR LIFESTYLE: Consider the lifestyle you want to maintain during retirement. This includes housing, travel, hobbies, and daily expenses.

- Determine Retirement Age: Decide when you plan to retire. This affects how much you need to save and the duration of your retirement.

- Identify Specific Goals: Identify any specific goals you have for retirement, such as traveling, purchasing a second home, or supporting family members.

3. Creating a Retirement Budget:

A RETIREMENT BUDGET helps you manage your finances and ensure that your income covers your expenses. It provides a roadmap for your spending and saving habits during retirement.

Steps to Create a Retirement Budget:

- ESTIMATE MONTHLY EXPENSES: Estimate your monthly expenses, including housing, utilities, groceries, transportation, healthcare, and entertainment. Consider any changes in expenses that may occur during retirement.

- Account for Inflation: Factor in inflation when estimating future expenses. The cost of living tends to increase over time, so it's important to account for inflation in your budget.

- Plan for Healthcare Costs: Include healthcare costs in your budget, including insurance premiums, out-of-pocket expenses, and potential long-term care needs.

- Review and Adjust: Regularly review and adjust your budget to reflect changes in your financial situation and goals.

4. Maximizing Retirement Savings:

MAXIMIZING YOUR RETIREMENT savings is crucial for ensuring financial security. Explore different retirement savings options and strategies to build a robust retirement fund.

Steps to Maximize Retirement Savings:

- CONTRIBUTE TO RETIREMENT Accounts: Contribute to retirement accounts such as 401(k)s, IRAs, and Roth IRAs. Take advantage of employer matching contributions and maximize your annual contributions.

- Diversify Investments: Diversify your investment portfolio to spread risk and increase potential returns. Consider a mix of stocks, bonds, mutual funds, and other investment vehicles.

- Automate Savings: Set up automatic contributions to your retirement accounts. Automating savings ensures consistent contributions and reduces the temptation to spend.

- Review and Rebalance: Regularly review and rebalance your investment portfolio to ensure it aligns with your retirement goals and risk tolerance.

5. Understanding Social Security Benefits:

SOCIAL SECURITY BENEFITS are an important source of income for many retirees. Understanding how Social Security works and planning when to start benefits can impact your financial security.

Steps to Understand Social Security Benefits:

- ESTIMATE BENEFITS: Use the Social Security Administration's online tools to estimate your benefits based on your earnings history and retirement age.

- Decide When to Start Benefits: Determine the best time to start receiving Social Security benefits. Starting benefits early reduces the monthly amount, while delaying benefits increases it.

- Consider Spousal Benefits: If you are married, consider spousal benefits. You may be eligible for benefits based on your spouse's earnings record.

6. Planning for Healthcare Costs:

HEALTHCARE COSTS ARE a significant consideration in retirement planning. Budgeting for healthcare expenses and exploring insurance options helps ensure you have adequate coverage.

Steps to Plan for Healthcare Costs:

- RESEARCH MEDICARE: Understand how Medicare works and what it covers. Consider additional coverage options such as Medigap policies or Medicare Advantage plans.

- Budget for Out-of-Pocket Expenses: Budget for out-of-pocket healthcare expenses, including copayments, deductibles, and non-covered services.

- Consider Long-Term Care Insurance: Explore long-term care insurance to cover the costs of long-term care services, such as nursing home care or in-home care.

Managing Finances and Budgeting

Effective management of your finances and budgeting is essential for maintaining financial stability during retirement. By creating a budget, tracking expenses, and managing debt, you can ensure that your retirement funds last and support your desired lifestyle.

Steps to Create a Budget:

1. Calculate Monthly Income:

START BY CALCULATING your monthly income from all sources, including pensions, Social Security, retirement accounts, investments, and part-time work.

Steps to Calculate Monthly Income:

- LIST INCOME SOURCES: List all sources of income, including fixed income (pensions, Social Security) and variable income (investment returns, part-time work).

- Estimate Monthly Amounts: Estimate the monthly amount you receive from each income source. Consider any seasonal or irregular income.

- Total Monthly Income: Add up the estimated monthly amounts to determine your total monthly income.

2. Identify Monthly Expenses:

IDENTIFY YOUR MONTHLY expenses, including essential expenses (housing, utilities, groceries) and discretionary expenses (entertainment, travel).

Steps to Identify Monthly Expenses:

- LIST ESSENTIAL EXPENSES: List essential expenses, such as housing (rent/mortgage, property taxes), utilities (electricity, water, gas), groceries, transportation, and healthcare.

- List Discretionary Expenses: List discretionary expenses, such as entertainment, dining out, travel, hobbies, and gifts.

- Estimate Monthly Amounts: Estimate the monthly amount you spend on each expense category. Use past spending records to make accurate estimates.

3. Create a Spending Plan:

CREATE A SPENDING PLAN that outlines how you will allocate your income to cover your expenses. Ensure that your spending plan aligns with your budget and financial goals.

Steps to Create a Spending Plan:

- PRIORITIZE ESSENTIAL Expenses: Prioritize essential expenses in your spending plan. Ensure that your income covers these expenses before allocating funds to discretionary spending.

- Allocate Funds to Discretionary Spending: Allocate funds to discretionary spending based on your priorities and financial goals. Be mindful of overspending in this category.

- Adjust as Needed: Regularly review and adjust your spending plan to reflect changes in your financial situation and goals.

Tracking Expenses and Managing Debt:

1. Track Your Spending:

TRACKING YOUR SPENDING helps you stay within your budget and identify areas where you can save. Use tools and methods that work best for you to monitor your expenses.

Steps to Track Your Spending:

- USE A BUDGETING APP: Use a budgeting app to track your spending and categorize expenses. Many apps sync with your bank accounts and provide real-time updates.

- Maintain a Spending Journal: Keep a spending journal to record your daily expenses. This method provides a detailed view of your spending habits.

- Review Bank Statements: Regularly review your bank statements to track your spending and identify any discrepancies.

2. Reduce and Manage Debt:

MANAGING DEBT IS CRUCIAL for financial stability in retirement. Reducing and eliminating debt frees up funds for other expenses and reduces financial stress.

Steps to Reduce and Manage Debt:

- PRIORITIZE HIGH-INTEREST Debt: Focus on paying off high-interest debt, such as credit card balances, first. High-interest debt can quickly accumulate and become unmanageable.

- Consolidate Debt: Consider consolidating debt into a single loan with a lower interest rate. This simplifies repayment and can reduce overall interest costs.

- Create a Repayment Plan: Create a debt repayment plan that outlines how much you will pay each month and when you expect to be debt-free.

- Avoid New Debt: Avoid taking on new debt unless absolutely necessary. Focus on living within your means and paying for expenses with available funds.

3. Save for Emergencies:

BUILDING AN EMERGENCY fund is essential for financial security. An emergency fund provides a safety net for unexpected expenses and reduces the need to rely on credit.

Steps to Save for Emergencies:

- SET A SAVINGS GOAL: Set a goal for your emergency fund, such as three to six months' worth of living expenses. This provides a cushion for unexpected events.

- Automate Savings: Automate contributions to your emergency fund. Set up automatic transfers from your checking account to a dedicated savings account.

- Use the Fund Wisely: Use your emergency fund only for genuine emergencies, such as medical expenses, car repairs, or home maintenance. Avoid dipping into the fund for non-essential expenses.

Legal Considerations: Wills, Trusts, and Healthcare Directives

Legal planning is an important aspect of financial security and peace of mind. Creating wills, trusts, and healthcare directives ensures that your wishes are honored and your loved ones are provided for in the event of incapacity or death.

Understanding Wills:

1. DEFINITION OF A Will:

A will is a legal document that outlines how your assets will be distributed after your death. It allows you to specify beneficiaries, appoint an executor, and make special bequests.

2. Importance of a Will:

Having a will ensures that your assets are distributed according to your wishes and reduces the potential for disputes among heirs. It provides clarity and guidance for your loved ones during a difficult time.

Steps to Create a Will:

1. List Your Assets:

START BY LISTING ALL your assets, including property, bank accounts, investments, personal belongings, and any other valuable items.

Steps to List Your Assets:

- CREATE AN INVENTORY: Create a detailed inventory of your assets. Include descriptions, locations, and approximate values.

- Include Digital Assets: Include digital assets, such as online accounts, social media profiles, and digital files. Provide instructions for accessing these assets.

2. Choose Beneficiaries:

CHOOSE BENEFICIARIES who will inherit your assets. Specify how your assets will be divided among your beneficiaries.

Steps to Choose Beneficiaries:

- IDENTIFY BENEFICIARIES: Identify the individuals or organizations you wish to benefit from your estate. These could include family members, friends, or charitable organizations.

- Specify Distribution: Specify how your assets will be distributed among your beneficiaries. Be clear and specific to avoid confusion or disputes.

3. Appoint an Executor:

APPOINT AN EXECUTOR who will be responsible for administering your estate and ensuring that your wishes are carried out.

Steps to Appoint an Executor:

- CHOOSE A TRUSTED INDIVIDUAL: Choose a trusted individual who is capable of handling the responsibilities of an executor. This could be a family member, friend, or professional advisor.

- Discuss the Role: Discuss the role and responsibilities with the chosen individual to ensure they are willing and able to serve as your executor.

4. Draft and Sign the Will:

DRAFT YOUR WILL WITH the help of an attorney or using a reputable online service. Ensure that the will is signed and witnessed according to your state's legal requirements.

Steps to Draft and Sign the Will:

- CONSULT AN ATTORNEY: Consult an attorney who specializes in estate planning to draft your will. An attorney can provide legal guidance and ensure that the will meets all legal requirements.

- Sign and Witness: Sign the will in the presence of witnesses. The number of witnesses and their qualifications may vary by state. Ensure that the will is properly witnessed and notarized if required.

5. Store the Will Safely:

STORE YOUR WILL IN a safe place and inform your executor and loved ones of its location. Consider keeping a copy with your attorney or in a secure online storage service.

Steps to Store the Will Safely:

- USE A SAFE: STORE the original will in a fireproof safe or secure location. Ensure that the safe is accessible to your executor.

- Inform Key Individuals: Inform your executor, attorney, and loved ones of the location of the will and how to access it. Provide copies if necessary.

Understanding Trusts:

1. DEFINITION OF A Trust:

A trust is a legal arrangement in which a trustee holds and manages assets on behalf of beneficiaries. Trusts can be used to manage assets during your lifetime and distribute them after your death.

2. Types of Trusts:

There are several types of trusts, each serving different purposes. Common types include revocable living trusts, irrevocable trusts, and special needs trusts.

Types of Trusts:

- Revocable Living Trust: A revocable living trust allows you to retain control over your assets during your lifetime and designate beneficiaries for after your death. You can amend or revoke the trust at any time.

- Irrevocable Trust: An irrevocable trust transfers ownership of assets to the trust permanently. The assets are no longer part of your estate, which can provide tax benefits and protection from creditors.

- Special Needs Trust: A special needs trust is designed to provide for a beneficiary with disabilities without affecting their eligibility for government benefits.

Steps to Create a Trust:

1. Determine Your Goals:

DETERMINE YOUR GOALS for creating a trust. Consider the type of trust that best meets your needs and objectives.

Steps to Determine Your Goals:

- ASSESS YOUR NEEDS: Assess your financial and estate planning needs. Consider factors such as asset protection, tax planning, and beneficiary considerations.

- Choose the Type of Trust: Choose the type of trust that aligns with your goals. Consult an attorney to understand the benefits and implications of each type of trust.

2. Select a Trustee:

SELECT A TRUSTEE WHO will manage the trust and its assets. The trustee can be an individual or a professional institution.

Steps to Select a Trustee:

- CHOOSE A TRUSTED INDIVIDUAL: Choose a trusted individual who is capable of managing the trust. This could be a family member, friend, or professional advisor.

- Consider a Professional Trustee: Consider appointing a professional trustee, such as a bank or trust company, if the trust is complex or if you prefer professional management.

3. Fund the Trust:

TRANSFER ASSETS INTO the trust. This process, known as funding the trust, involves retitling assets in the name of the trust.

Steps to Fund the Trust:

- RETITLE ASSETS: RETITLE assets, such as real estate, bank accounts, and investments, in the name of the trust. Consult an attorney or financial advisor for guidance.

- Transfer Ownership: Transfer ownership of personal property, such as vehicles or valuable items, to the trust. Provide documentation to the trustee.

4. Draft and Sign the Trust Document:

DRAFT THE TRUST DOCUMENT with the help of an attorney. Ensure that the trust document is signed and witnessed according to legal requirements.

Steps to Draft and Sign the Trust Document:

- CONSULT AN ATTORNEY: Consult an attorney who specializes in trust and estate planning to draft the trust document. An attorney can provide legal guidance and ensure that the document meets all legal requirements.

- Sign and Witness: Sign the trust document in the presence of witnesses. The number of witnesses and their qualifications may vary by state. Ensure that the document is properly witnessed and notarized if required.

5. Review and Update the Trust:

REGULARLY REVIEW AND update the trust to reflect changes in your financial situation, goals, or beneficiaries. Ensure that the trust remains aligned with your estate planning objectives.

Steps to Review and Update the Trust:

- SCHEDULE REGULAR REVIEWS: Schedule regular reviews of the trust with your attorney. Review the trust document and funding to ensure they are up-to-date.

- Amend as Needed: Amend the trust document to reflect changes in your financial situation, goals, or beneficiaries. Ensure that any amendments are properly documented and signed.

Understanding Healthcare Directives:

1. DEFINITION OF HEALTHCARE Directives:

Healthcare directives are legal documents that outline your wishes for medical treatment and appoint someone to make healthcare decisions on your behalf if you are unable to do so.

2. Types of Healthcare Directives:

Common types of healthcare directives include living wills, durable power of attorney for healthcare, and Do Not Resuscitate (DNR) orders.

Types of Healthcare Directives:

- Living Will: A living will outlines your preferences for medical treatment in the event that you are unable to communicate your wishes. It typically covers decisions about life-sustaining treatment, resuscitation, and organ donation.

- Durable Power of Attorney for Healthcare: A durable power of attorney for healthcare appoints a healthcare agent to make medical decisions on your behalf if you are incapacitated. The agent should be someone you trust to act in accordance with your wishes.

- Do Not Resuscitate (DNR) Order: A DNR order instructs medical personnel not to perform cardiopulmonary resuscitation (CPR) if your heart stops. It is typically used for individuals with terminal illnesses or advanced directives.

Steps to Create Healthcare Directives:

1. Determine Your Wishes:

DETERMINE YOUR WISHES for medical treatment and end-of-life care. Consider factors such as resuscitation, life-sustaining treatment, and organ donation.

Steps to Determine Your Wishes:

- REFLECT ON VALUES: Reflect on your values and beliefs about medical treatment and end-of-life care. Consider what is most important to you in terms of quality of life and medical intervention.

- Discuss with Loved Ones: Discuss your wishes with loved ones to ensure they understand your preferences and can support your decisions.

2. Appoint a Healthcare Agent:

APPOINT A HEALTHCARE agent who will make medical decisions on your behalf if you are unable to do so. Choose someone you trust to act in accordance with your wishes.

Steps to Appoint a Healthcare Agent:

- CHOOSE A TRUSTED INDIVIDUAL: Choose a trusted individual, such as a family member or close friend, who is willing and able to act as your healthcare agent.

- Discuss the Role: Discuss the role and responsibilities with the chosen individual to ensure they understand and are willing to serve as your healthcare agent.

3. Draft and Sign Healthcare Directives:

DRAFT HEALTHCARE DIRECTIVES with the help of an attorney or using a reputable online service. Ensure that the documents are signed and witnessed according to legal requirements.

Steps to Draft and Sign Healthcare Directives:

- CONSULT AN ATTORNEY: Consult an attorney who specializes in estate planning to draft healthcare directives. An attorney can provide legal guidance and ensure that the documents meet all legal requirements.

- Sign and Witness: Sign the healthcare directives in the presence of witnesses. The number of witnesses and their qualifications may vary by state. Ensure that the documents are properly witnessed and notarized if required.

4. Distribute Copies:

DISTRIBUTE COPIES OF your healthcare directives to your healthcare agent, loved ones, and healthcare providers. Ensure that key individuals have access to the documents in an emergency.

Steps to Distribute Copies:

- PROVIDE COPIES TO Key Individuals: Provide copies of your healthcare directives to your healthcare agent, family members, and healthcare providers. Ensure they understand your wishes and know where to find the documents.

- Store Documents Safely: Store the original documents in a safe place that is easily accessible to your healthcare agent and loved ones. Consider keeping copies with your attorney or in a secure online storage service.

Case Studies: Financial Security and Planning

Case Study 1: Sarah's Journey to Financial Stability

Sarah, a 65-year-old retiree, took proactive steps to ensure her financial security during retirement.

Sarah's Strategies:

- ASSESSING FINANCIAL Situation: Sarah assessed her financial situation by tracking her income, expenses, and savings. She calculated her net worth to understand her financial health.

- Setting Retirement Goals: Sarah set clear retirement goals, including maintaining her current lifestyle, traveling, and supporting her grandchildren's education.

- Creating a Retirement Budget: Sarah created a detailed retirement budget that accounted for essential and discretionary expenses. She included healthcare costs and factored in inflation.

- Maximizing Retirement Savings: Sarah contributed to her retirement accounts, diversified her investments, and set up automatic savings. She regularly reviewed and rebalanced her portfolio.

- Understanding Social Security Benefits: Sarah used online tools to estimate her Social Security benefits and decided to delay benefits until age 70 to maximize her monthly amount.

- Planning for Healthcare Costs: Sarah researched Medicare and supplemental insurance options. She budgeted for out-of-pocket expenses and considered long-term care insurance.

Results:

Through her proactive financial planning efforts, Sarah achieved financial stability and peace of mind. She was able to maintain her desired lifestyle, cover healthcare costs, and enjoy her retirement without financial stress. Sarah's journey highlighted the importance of comprehensive financial planning for retirement.

Case Study 2: John's Path to Estate Planning

JOHN, A 70-YEAR-OLD retired engineer, focused on estate planning to ensure his wishes were honored and his loved ones were provided for.

John's Strategies:

- CREATING A WILL: JOHN listed his assets, chose beneficiaries, and appointed an executor. He worked with an attorney to draft and sign his will, ensuring it met legal requirements.

- Establishing a Trust: John established a revocable living trust to manage his assets and provide for his family. He selected a trustee, funded the trust, and regularly reviewed and updated the trust document.

- Drafting Healthcare Directives: John determined his wishes for medical treatment and end-of-life care. He appointed a healthcare agent, drafted healthcare directives, and distributed copies to key individuals.

- Managing Finances: John created a budget, tracked his expenses, and managed his debt. He built an emergency fund and avoided taking on new debt.

Results:

By focusing on estate planning and financial management, John ensured that his wishes were honored and his loved ones were provided for. He achieved peace of mind knowing that his estate was in order and his healthcare preferences were documented. John's path demonstrated the importance of legal considerations and financial planning for overall well-being.

Conclusion

Financial security and planning are essential components of aging well. By understanding the importance of financial planning for retirement, effectively managing finances and budgeting, and addressing legal considerations such as wills, trusts, and healthcare directives, you can ensure a stable and fulfilling retirement.

In this chapter, we explored the steps to effective financial planning, strategies for managing finances and budgeting, and the critical legal considerations for ensuring your wishes are honored. By integrating these practices into your life, you can achieve financial security, reduce stress, and enjoy a fulfilling and enriched retirement.

As you continue to explore the strategies for mind, body, and spirit outlined in this book, remember that financial security and planning are crucial aspects of living your best life at any age. Embrace the journey of aging with a proactive and positive attitude, and prioritize your financial well-being to enjoy a long, healthy, and fulfilling life.

Chapter 8: Navigating Healthcare Systems

Understanding Healthcare Options and Insurance

Navigating the healthcare system can be complex, especially as we age and our healthcare needs become more varied. Understanding the different healthcare options and insurance plans available is crucial for accessing the care you need and managing your healthcare costs effectively.

Healthcare Options:

1. Primary Care:

PRIMARY CARE PROVIDERS (PCPs) are your first point of contact for general health concerns. They provide preventive care, diagnose and treat common illnesses, and manage chronic conditions.

Types of Primary Care Providers:

- FAMILY PHYSICIANS: Treat patients of all ages and provide comprehensive care.

- Internists: Specialize in the care of adults and manage a wide range of health issues.

- Geriatricians: Focus on the healthcare needs of older adults.

- Nurse Practitioners (NPs) and Physician Assistants (PAs): Provide care under the supervision of a physician and can diagnose and treat illnesses, prescribe medications, and manage chronic conditions.

2. Specialty Care:

SPECIALISTS PROVIDE care for specific health conditions that require expertise beyond primary care. Examples include cardiologists, endocrinologists, orthopedists, and oncologists.

When to See a Specialist:

- REFERRAL FROM PCP: Your primary care provider may refer you to a specialist if you have a condition that requires specialized knowledge or treatment.

- Self-Referral: In some cases, you may choose to see a specialist directly, especially if your insurance plan allows it.

3. Hospitals and Emergency Care:

HOSPITALS PROVIDE A range of services, including emergency care, surgery, inpatient care, and specialized treatments. Emergency rooms (ERs) are equipped to handle acute and life-threatening conditions.

When to Seek Emergency Care:

- LIFE-THREATENING CONDITIONS: Seek emergency care for conditions such as heart attacks, strokes, severe injuries, or difficulty breathing.

- Urgent Conditions: For urgent but non-life-threatening conditions, consider urgent care centers, which provide prompt care for issues like minor injuries, infections, and sudden illnesses.

4. Long-Term Care:

LONG-TERM CARE INCLUDES services and support for individuals with chronic health conditions or disabilities. It can be provided at home, in assisted living facilities, or in nursing homes.

Types of Long-Term Care:

- HOME CARE: SERVICES provided in the patient's home, such as personal care, nursing care, and therapy.

- Assisted Living: Residential facilities that provide personal care, meals, and social activities for individuals who need help with daily activities.

- Nursing Homes: Facilities that provide medical and personal care for individuals with significant health needs.

Understanding Healthcare Insurance:

1. MEDICARE:

Medicare is a federal health insurance program primarily for individuals aged 65 and older, as well as for some younger individuals with disabilities.

Components of Medicare:

- MEDICARE PART A: HOSPITAL insurance that covers inpatient hospital stays, skilled nursing facility care, hospice care, and some home health care.

- Medicare Part B: Medical insurance that covers outpatient care, doctor visits, preventive services, and some home health care.

- Medicare Part C (Medicare Advantage): Plans offered by private insurers that provide Part A and Part B benefits, often with additional services such as vision, dental, and prescription drug coverage.

- Medicare Part D: Prescription drug coverage offered by private insurers to help cover the cost of prescription medications.

Steps to Enroll in Medicare:

- INITIAL ENROLLMENT Period: Enroll during the seven-month period that begins three months before your 65th birthday, includes your birth month, and ends three months after your birthday.

- Special Enrollment Period: Enroll outside the initial enrollment period if you qualify due to certain life events, such as losing employer coverage.

- Annual Enrollment Period: Make changes to your Medicare plan during the annual open enrollment period from October 15 to December 7 each year.

2. Medicaid:

Medicaid is a joint federal and state program that provides health coverage for low-income individuals and families. Eligibility and benefits vary by state.

Eligibility for Medicaid:

- INCOME AND RESOURCES: Eligibility is based on income and resource limits set by each state.

- Categorical Eligibility: Certain groups, such as pregnant women, children, and individuals with disabilities, may qualify based on specific criteria.

Steps to Apply for Medicaid:

- CHECK ELIGIBILITY: Visit your state's Medicaid website or contact your local Medicaid office to check eligibility criteria.

- Submit an Application: Complete and submit an application online, by mail, or in person at your local Medicaid office.

3. Private Health Insurance:

PRIVATE HEALTH INSURANCE is offered by employers, purchased individually, or obtained through the Health Insurance Marketplace.

Types of Private Health Insurance Plans:

- HEALTH MAINTENANCE Organization (HMO): Requires you to choose a primary care provider and get referrals to see specialists. Offers lower premiums and out-of-pocket costs but limited provider networks.

- Preferred Provider Organization (PPO): Allows you to see any healthcare provider without a referral. Offers more flexibility but may have higher premiums and out-of-pocket costs.

- Exclusive Provider Organization (EPO): Similar to an HMO but does not require referrals. You must use network providers except in emergencies.

- Point of Service (POS): Combines features of HMOs and PPOs. Requires a primary care provider and referrals but allows out-of-network care at higher costs.

Steps to Choose a Private Health Insurance Plan:

- COMPARE PLANS: USE the Health Insurance Marketplace or other comparison tools to compare plan options, coverage, and costs.

- Consider Your Needs: Evaluate your healthcare needs, including preferred providers, medications, and potential medical expenses.

- Check Provider Networks: Ensure that your preferred doctors and hospitals are in the plan's network.

- Review Costs: Consider premiums, deductibles, copayments, and coinsurance to understand the total cost of the plan.

4. Supplemental Insurance:

SUPPLEMENTAL INSURANCE, such as Medigap and long-term care insurance, provides additional coverage to help pay for costs not covered by Medicare or other health insurance plans.

Types of Supplemental Insurance:

- MEDIGAP: PRIVATE INSURANCE that helps cover out-of-pocket costs not covered by Medicare, such as copayments, coinsurance, and deductibles. Available to individuals enrolled in Medicare Part A and Part B.

- Long-Term Care Insurance: Provides coverage for long-term care services, including home care, assisted living, and nursing home care. Helps protect savings and assets from the high costs of long-term care.

Steps to Choose Supplemental Insurance:

- ASSESS YOUR NEEDS: Evaluate your healthcare needs and financial situation to determine the type and level of coverage you need.

- Compare Policies: Compare policies from different insurers, considering coverage, costs, and exclusions.

- Review Ratings: Check ratings and reviews from independent organizations, such as the National Association of Insurance Commissioners (NAIC) and A.M. Best.

Communicating Effectively with Healthcare Providers

Effective communication with healthcare providers is essential for receiving the best possible care. Clear and open communication helps ensure that your healthcare needs and preferences are understood and addressed.

Steps to Communicate Effectively with Healthcare Providers:

1. Prepare for Appointments:

PREPARATION HELPS YOU make the most of your time with healthcare providers and ensures that all important issues are discussed.

Steps to Prepare for Appointments:

- MAKE A LIST OF QUESTIONS: Write down any questions or concerns you have before your appointment. Prioritize the most important issues to discuss.

- Bring Medical Records: Bring relevant medical records, including test results, medication lists, and previous diagnoses, to provide your provider with a complete picture of your health.

- Note Symptoms: Keep a record of any symptoms you are experiencing, including when they started, how often they occur, and any factors that worsen or improve them.

2. Ask Questions:

Asking questions helps you understand your diagnosis, treatment options, and overall health. Don't hesitate to ask for clarification if something is unclear.

Questions to Ask Healthcare Providers:

- ABOUT YOUR DIAGNOSIS: What is my diagnosis? What caused this condition? How will it affect my health?

- About Treatment Options: What are my treatment options? What are the benefits and risks of each option? How effective are they?

- About Medications: What medications are prescribed? How should I take them? Are there any side effects or interactions with other medications?

- About Follow-Up Care: What follow-up care is needed? When should I schedule my next appointment? Are there any lifestyle changes I should make?

3. Be Honest and Open:

HONESTY IS CRUCIAL for effective communication. Provide complete and accurate information about your health, lifestyle, and any challenges you face.

Steps to Be Honest and Open:

- SHARE YOUR CONCERNS: Discuss any concerns or worries you have about your health or treatment. Your provider can address these concerns and provide support.

- Discuss Lifestyle Factors: Share information about your diet, exercise habits, smoking, alcohol consumption, and other lifestyle factors that may impact your health.

- Report All Symptoms: Report all symptoms, even if they seem minor or unrelated. This helps your provider make an accurate diagnosis and develop an appropriate treatment plan.

4. Take Notes:

TAKING NOTES DURING your appointment helps you remember important information and instructions. You can also bring a trusted friend or family member to help you take notes and ask questions.

Steps to Take Notes:

- WRITE DOWN KEY POINTS: Write down key points from your discussion, including your diagnosis, treatment plan, and any instructions or recommendations.

- Review Your Notes: Review your notes after the appointment to ensure you understand and remember the information. If anything is unclear, contact your provider for clarification.

5. Advocate for Yourself:

ADVOCACY INVOLVES ACTIVELY participating in your healthcare and ensuring that your needs and preferences are respected. Don't be afraid to speak up and ask for what you need.

Steps to Advocate for Yourself:

- EXPRESS YOUR PREFERENCES: Clearly express your preferences and values regarding your care. This helps your provider tailor the treatment plan to your needs.

- Ask for a Second Opinion: If you have concerns about your diagnosis or treatment plan, don't hesitate to ask for a second opinion from another healthcare provider.

- Use Patient Resources: Utilize patient resources, such as patient advocates, support groups, and educational materials, to support your advocacy efforts.

6. Follow Up:

FOLLOWING UP AFTER your appointment ensures that you understand and adhere to your treatment plan. It also provides an opportunity to address any new or ongoing concerns.

Steps to Follow Up:

- SCHEDULE FOLLOW-UP Appointments: Schedule follow-up appointments as recommended by your provider. Keep track of appointment dates and any necessary preparations.

- Monitor Your Progress: Monitor your progress and any changes in your symptoms or health. Keep a record of this information to discuss at your next appointment.

- Contact Your Provider: Contact your provider if you have any questions, concerns, or side effects related to your treatment. Don't wait until your next appointment to address urgent issues.

Making Informed Healthcare Decisions

Making informed healthcare decisions involves understanding your options, considering your preferences and values, and collaborating with your healthcare providers. Informed decision-making empowers you to take control of your health and receive the best possible care.

Steps to Make Informed Healthcare Decisions:

1. Gather Information:

GATHERING ACCURATE and reliable information about your health condition, treatment options, and potential outcomes is essential for informed decision-making.

Steps to Gather Information:

- CONSULT YOUR HEALTHCARE Provider: Ask your healthcare provider for detailed information about your diagnosis, treatment options, and expected outcomes. Request written materials or reputable websites for further reading.

- Use Trusted Sources: Use trusted sources of medical information, such as government health websites (e.g., CDC, NIH), academic institutions, and reputable medical organizations (e.g., American Heart Association, Mayo Clinic).

- Read Patient Reviews: Read patient reviews and testimonials to gain insights into the experiences of others who have undergone similar treatments or procedures.

2. Evaluate Treatment Options:

EVALUATE THE AVAILABLE treatment options, considering their benefits, risks, and potential impact on your quality of life.

Steps to Evaluate Treatment Options:

- COMPARE BENEFITS AND Risks: Compare the benefits and risks of each treatment option. Consider factors such as effectiveness, side effects, recovery time, and potential complications.

- Consider Quality of Life: Assess how each treatment option may affect your quality of life, including physical, emotional, and social aspects. Consider your ability to perform daily activities, maintain independence, and enjoy your hobbies and interests.

- Review Alternatives: Explore alternative treatments or complementary therapies that may be available. Discuss these options with your healthcare provider to understand their potential benefits and limitations.

3. Consider Your Preferences and Values:

YOUR PREFERENCES AND values play a crucial role in decision-making. Consider what matters most to you in terms of your health, lifestyle, and personal goals.

Steps to Consider Your Preferences and Values:

- REFLECT ON YOUR GOALS: Reflect on your short-term and long-term health goals. Consider what you hope to achieve through treatment and what outcomes are most important to you.

- Identify Your Values: Identify your core values, such as maintaining independence, minimizing pain, or prioritizing family time. Use these values to guide your decision-making process.

- Discuss with Loved Ones: Discuss your preferences and values with your loved ones. Their support and understanding can help you make decisions that align with your goals and values.

4. Collaborate with Your Healthcare Provider:

COLLABORATION WITH your healthcare provider ensures that your decisions are informed by medical expertise and tailored to your needs.

Steps to Collaborate with Your Healthcare Provider:

- SHARE YOUR PREFERENCES: Share your preferences and values with your healthcare provider. Discuss how these factors influence your treatment choices.

- Ask for Recommendations: Ask your provider for recommendations based on your medical history, diagnosis, and personal goals. Seek their input on the best course of action.

- Discuss Potential Outcomes: Discuss the potential outcomes of each treatment option, including best-case and worst-case scenarios. This helps you set realistic expectations and make informed choices.

5. Make a Decision:

ONCE YOU HAVE GATHERED information, evaluated options, and considered your preferences, make a decision that aligns with your goals and values.

Steps to Make a Decision:

- WEIGH THE PROS AND Cons: Weigh the pros and cons of each option, considering the information and input from your healthcare provider.

- Trust Your Instincts: Trust your instincts and intuition. You know your body and your needs best, so make a decision that feels right for you.

- Be Confident: Be confident in your decision. Remember that you have taken a thoughtful and informed approach to making the best choice for your health.

6. Review and Adjust as Needed:

HEALTHCARE DECISIONS are not always final. Regularly review and adjust your treatment plan as needed based on your progress and any new information.

Steps to Review and Adjust:

- MONITOR YOUR PROGRESS: Monitor your progress and any changes in your symptoms or health. Keep a record of this information to discuss with your provider.

- Communicate with Your Provider: Maintain open communication with your healthcare provider. Share any concerns or changes in your condition and seek their guidance on adjustments to your treatment plan.

- Stay Informed: Stay informed about new developments in medical research and treatment options. This helps you make timely adjustments to your healthcare decisions.

Case Studies: Navigating Healthcare Systems

Case Study 1: Emily's Journey to Effective Communication

Emily, a 70-year-old retired teacher, struggled with managing her chronic health conditions and communicating effectively with her healthcare providers.

Emily's Strategies:

- PREPARING FOR APPOINTMENTS: Emily prepared for her appointments by making a list of questions and concerns, bringing her medical records, and noting her symptoms.

- Asking Questions: During her appointments, Emily asked questions about her diagnosis, treatment options, and medications. She sought clarification when needed and took notes to remember important information.

- Being Honest and Open: Emily was honest and open with her healthcare providers about her lifestyle, symptoms, and challenges. She shared her concerns and discussed any difficulties she faced in adhering to her treatment plan.

- Advocating for Herself: Emily advocated for herself by expressing her preferences and values, asking for a second opinion when necessary, and utilizing patient resources for additional support.

Results:

Through her proactive approach to communication, Emily built strong relationships with her healthcare providers and received personalized care that addressed her needs and preferences. Emily's journey highlighted the importance of effective communication in navigating the healthcare system.

Case Study 2: John's Path to Informed Decision-Making

JOHN, A 68-YEAR-OLD retired engineer, faced a difficult decision regarding treatment for a newly diagnosed health condition.

John's Strategies:

- GATHERING INFORMATION: John gathered information about his condition and treatment options from his healthcare provider, reputable medical websites, and patient reviews. He sought detailed information about the benefits and risks of each option.

- Evaluating Treatment Options: John evaluated the available treatment options, considering their effectiveness, side effects, recovery time, and impact on his quality of life.

- Considering Preferences and Values: John reflected on his health goals and core values, prioritizing treatments that would allow him to maintain his independence and enjoy his hobbies.

- Collaborating with His Provider: John collaborated with his healthcare provider, sharing his preferences and values, and seeking their recommendations. He discussed potential outcomes and set realistic expectations.

- Making a Decision: After weighing the pros and cons and trusting his instincts, John made an informed decision that aligned with his goals and values.

Results:

By taking a thoughtful and informed approach to decision-making, John received a treatment plan that met his needs and supported his overall well-being. John's path demonstrated the importance of gathering information, evaluating options, and collaborating with healthcare providers in making healthcare decisions.

Conclusion

Navigating healthcare systems is essential for accessing the care you need and managing your healthcare effectively. By understanding healthcare options and insurance, communicating effectively with healthcare providers, and making informed healthcare decisions, you can ensure that your healthcare needs are met and your well-being is prioritized.

In this chapter, we explored the importance of understanding healthcare options and insurance, strategies for effective communication with healthcare providers, and steps for making informed healthcare decisions. By integrating these practices into your healthcare journey, you can achieve better health outcomes, reduce stress, and enjoy a higher quality of life.

As you continue to explore the strategies for mind, body, and spirit outlined in this book, remember that navigating healthcare systems is a crucial aspect of living your best life at any age. Embrace the journey of aging with a proactive and positive attitude, and prioritize your healthcare needs to enjoy a long, healthy, and fulfilling life.

Chapter 9: Staying Active and Engaged

Benefits of Staying Physically Active

Staying physically active is crucial for maintaining health, vitality, and overall well-being as we age. Regular physical activity provides numerous benefits, including improved physical health, mental well-being, and enhanced quality of life. In this section, we will explore the benefits of staying physically active, provide practical tips for incorporating exercise into daily life, and highlight specific exercises that are particularly beneficial for older adults.

Benefits of Regular Physical Activity:

1. IMPROVED CARDIOVASCULAR Health:

Regular exercise strengthens the heart and improves circulation, reducing the risk of cardiovascular diseases such as heart attacks and strokes. Activities like walking, swimming, and cycling help maintain a healthy heart.

2. Enhanced Muscular Strength and Flexibility:

Physical activity helps maintain muscle mass, strength, and flexibility, which are essential for daily activities and independence. Strength training exercises, such as lifting weights or using resistance bands, can prevent muscle loss and improve mobility.

3. Better Bone Health:

Weight-bearing exercises, such as walking, jogging, and strength training, help maintain bone density and reduce the risk of osteoporosis and fractures. Strong bones support overall mobility and prevent injuries.

4. Weight Management:

Regular physical activity helps control body weight by burning calories and increasing metabolism. Maintaining a healthy weight reduces the risk of chronic conditions such as diabetes, hypertension, and heart disease.

5. Improved Mental Health:

Exercise is known to boost mood and reduce symptoms of depression and anxiety. Physical activity stimulates the production of endorphins, the body's natural mood elevators, and helps alleviate stress.

6. Enhanced Cognitive Function:

Regular exercise has been linked to improved cognitive function and a reduced risk of cognitive decline and dementia. Physical activity increases blood flow to the brain, supporting brain health and enhancing memory and thinking skills.

7. Better Sleep:

Physical activity can improve sleep quality by helping you fall asleep faster and enjoy deeper sleep. Regular exercise also helps regulate your sleep-wake cycle.

8. Increased Energy Levels:

Regular physical activity boosts energy levels by improving cardiovascular health and enhancing muscular strength. It helps you feel more energetic and capable of performing daily activities.

9. Social Connection:

Participating in group exercise classes, sports, or community fitness activities provides opportunities for social interaction and builds a sense of community. Social connections are vital for emotional well-being and mental health.

Incorporating Exercise into Daily Life:

1. Start Slowly:

IF YOU ARE NEW TO EXERCISE or have been inactive for a while, start slowly and gradually increase the intensity and duration of your workouts. Listen to your body and avoid overexertion.

Steps to Start Slowly:

- BEGIN WITH LOW-IMPACT Activities: Start with low-impact activities such as walking, swimming, or gentle yoga. These activities are easy on the joints and provide a good foundation for more intense exercises.

- Set Realistic Goals: Set achievable goals based on your current fitness level. For example, aim to walk for 10 minutes a day and gradually increase the duration as you build endurance.

- Progress Gradually: Gradually increase the intensity and duration of your workouts as your fitness improves. Avoid sudden increases in activity levels to prevent injury.

2. Find Activities You Enjoy:

CHOOSE ACTIVITIES THAT you enjoy and look forward to doing. Enjoyable activities are more likely to become regular habits and contribute to long-term adherence to an active lifestyle.

Steps to Find Activities You Enjoy:

- EXPLORE DIFFERENT Activities: Try different types of physical activities to find what you enjoy most. Experiment with walking, dancing, swimming, cycling, gardening, or group exercise classes.

- Join a Group or Class: Join a fitness group or class that interests you. Group activities provide motivation, social interaction, and a sense of community.

- Make It Fun: Incorporate fun elements into your workouts, such as listening to music, exercising outdoors, or participating in recreational sports.

3. Create a Routine:

ESTABLISH A REGULAR exercise routine that fits into your daily schedule. Consistency is key to reaping the benefits of regular physical activity.

Steps to Create a Routine:

- SCHEDULE EXERCISE: Set aside specific times for exercise each day or week. Treat these times as important appointments and prioritize them.

- Mix It Up: Include a variety of exercises in your routine to keep it interesting and engage different muscle groups. Alternate between aerobic, strength, flexibility, and balance exercises.

- Be Flexible: While consistency is important, be flexible and adjust your routine as needed. If you miss a workout, don't get discouraged—just get back on track the next day.

4. Incorporate Physical Activity into Daily Tasks:

LOOK FOR OPPORTUNITIES to incorporate physical activity into your daily tasks and routines. Small changes can add up to significant health benefits over time.

Steps to Incorporate Physical Activity into Daily Tasks:

- TAKE THE STAIRS: OPT for stairs instead of elevators or escalators whenever possible. Climbing stairs is a great way to get your heart rate up and strengthen your legs.

- Walk More: Make walking a part of your daily routine. Walk to nearby destinations, take a stroll during breaks, or go for a walk after meals.

- Stay Active at Home: Engage in activities that keep you moving at home, such as gardening, housework, or playing with pets. These activities contribute to overall physical activity levels.

5. Track Your Progress:

TRACKING YOUR PROGRESS helps you stay motivated and monitor your improvements. Use tools and methods that work best for you to keep track of your activity levels.

Steps to Track Your Progress:

- KEEP A JOURNAL: MAINTAIN a journal to record your workouts, including the type of activity, duration, and intensity. Note any changes in how you feel or improvements in your fitness.

- Use a Fitness Tracker: Use a fitness tracker or smartphone app to monitor your activity levels, steps, and calories burned. These devices provide real-time feedback and motivation.

- Set Milestones: Set milestones and celebrate your achievements along the way. Recognizing your progress boosts motivation and encourages continued effort.

Specific Exercises for Older Adults:

1. Aerobic Exercises:

AEROBIC EXERCISES IMPROVE cardiovascular health and endurance. Aim for at least 150 minutes of moderate-intensity aerobic exercise per week.

Examples of Aerobic Exercises:

- WALKING: WALKING IS a low-impact and accessible exercise that can be done anywhere. Aim for brisk walking to get your heart rate up.

- Swimming: Swimming provides a full-body workout without putting stress on the joints. It's ideal for individuals with arthritis or mobility issues.

- Cycling: Cycling, whether on a stationary bike or outdoors, improves cardiovascular health and leg strength. Adjust the resistance to match your fitness level.

2. Strength Training Exercises:

STRENGTH TRAINING EXERCISES build and maintain muscle mass, improve bone density, and enhance overall strength. Aim to include strength training exercises at least two days per week.

Examples of Strength Training Exercises:

- WEIGHTLIFTING: USE free weights or weight machines to perform exercises such as bicep curls, bench presses, and leg presses. Start with light weights and gradually increase as you gain strength.

- Resistance Bands: Resistance bands provide a versatile and portable option for strength training. Use bands to perform exercises like squats, rows, and chest presses.

- Bodyweight Exercises: Bodyweight exercises, such as push-ups, squats, and lunges, use your body weight as resistance. These exercises can be modified to suit your fitness level.

3. Flexibility Exercises:

FLEXIBILITY EXERCISES improve the range of motion in your joints and muscles, enhancing mobility and reducing stiffness. Incorporate stretching and flexibility exercises into your routine several times per week.

Examples of Flexibility Exercises:

- STRETCHING: PERFORM static stretching exercises for major muscle groups, holding each stretch for 15-30 seconds. Focus on areas like the hamstrings, quadriceps, calves, and shoulders.

- Yoga: Yoga combines stretching with mindfulness and relaxation. Practice yoga poses that improve flexibility, such as downward dog, cat-cow, and seated forward bend.

- Tai Chi: Tai chi is a gentle martial art that emphasizes slow, flowing movements and deep breathing. It improves flexibility, balance, and relaxation.

4. Balance Exercises:

BALANCE EXERCISES ENHANCE stability and prevent falls. Incorporate balance exercises into your routine at least two to three times per week.

Examples of Balance Exercises:

- SINGLE-LEG STAND: Stand on one leg while holding onto a sturdy surface for support. Gradually increase the duration and try balancing without support.

- Heel-to-Toe Walk: Walk in a straight line, placing the heel of one foot directly in front of the toes of the other foot. This exercise improves coordination and balance.

- Tai Chi: Tai chi also serves as an excellent balance exercise, as it requires controlled movements and shifts in weight.

Social Activities and Community Involvement

Staying socially active and involved in the community is vital for emotional well-being, mental health, and overall life satisfaction. Social activities provide opportunities for connection, support, and engagement, helping to reduce feelings of isolation and loneliness.

Benefits of Social Activities and Community Involvement:

1. ENHANCED EMOTIONAL Well-Being:

Social interactions and connections provide emotional support, reduce stress, and improve mood. Being part of a community fosters a sense of belonging and purpose.

2. Mental Stimulation:

Engaging in social activities stimulates the mind and keeps it active. Conversations, group activities, and shared experiences provide mental challenges and promote cognitive health.

3. Physical Health Benefits:

Social activities often involve physical movement, such as dancing, walking, or group sports. These activities contribute to overall physical health and fitness.

4. Support Networks:

Building and maintaining social connections create a support network that can provide assistance, encouragement, and companionship during challenging times.

5. Increased Longevity:

Studies have shown that individuals who are socially active and engaged tend to live longer and enjoy better health than those who are isolated.

Ways to Stay Socially Active and Involved:

1. Join Social Clubs and Groups:

SOCIAL CLUBS AND GROUPS provide opportunities to meet new people, share interests, and participate in group activities.

Examples of Social Clubs and Groups:

- BOOK CLUBS: JOIN A book club to discuss and share your love of reading with others. Book clubs provide intellectual stimulation and foster meaningful conversations.

- Hobby Groups: Participate in hobby groups that align with your interests, such as gardening, knitting, painting, or photography. These groups offer a platform to share skills and learn from others.

- Sports and Recreation Clubs: Join sports and recreation clubs, such as walking groups, tennis clubs, or bowling leagues. These clubs promote physical activity and social interaction.

2. Volunteer in the Community:

VOLUNTEERING PROVIDES a sense of purpose and allows you to give back to the community. It also offers opportunities to meet new people and develop new skills.

Ways to Volunteer:

- LOCAL ORGANIZATIONS: Volunteer with local organizations, such as food banks, shelters, hospitals, or schools. Find causes that resonate with you and align with your values.

- Community Events: Participate in community events, such as festivals, fairs, or fundraisers. Volunteering at events helps you connect with others and contribute to community spirit.

- Mentorship Programs: Become a mentor for young people or peers. Sharing your knowledge and experience can have a positive impact on others and create lasting connections.

3. Participate in Religious or Spiritual Groups:

RELIGIOUS OR SPIRITUAL groups provide a sense of community and shared values. They offer opportunities for worship, study, and social activities.

Examples of Religious or Spiritual Activities:

- WORSHIP SERVICES: Attend regular worship services to connect with others who share your faith and values.

- Study Groups: Join study groups or classes to deepen your understanding of your faith and engage in meaningful discussions.

- Community Service: Participate in community service projects organized by your religious or spiritual group. These activities foster a sense of purpose and connection.

4. Attend Community Centers and Senior Centers:

COMMUNITY CENTERS AND senior centers offer a variety of programs and activities for older adults. These centers provide a space for socializing, learning, and staying active.

Activities at Community and Senior Centers:

- EXERCISE CLASSES: Participate in exercise classes, such as yoga, tai chi, or dance, offered at community and senior centers.

- Educational Programs: Attend educational programs, workshops, or lectures on topics of interest. These programs provide opportunities for lifelong learning.

- Social Events: Join social events, such as game nights, potlucks, or movie screenings, to connect with others and have fun.

5. Engage in Intergenerational Activities:

INTERGENERATIONAL ACTIVITIES involve interactions between different age groups, fostering understanding and connections across generations.

Examples of Intergenerational Activities:

- FAMILY ACTIVITIES: Spend time with family members of all ages, from grandchildren to elderly relatives. Participate in activities that everyone enjoys, such as family outings, game nights, or cooking together.

- Community Programs: Get involved in community programs that bring together different generations, such as intergenerational mentoring, gardening projects, or art collaborations.

- Educational Initiatives: Participate in educational initiatives that pair older adults with younger students for tutoring, storytelling, or cultural exchange programs.

Lifelong Learning and Pursuing Hobbies

Lifelong learning and pursuing hobbies are essential for mental stimulation, personal growth, and overall fulfillment. Engaging in continuous learning and exploring new interests enriches life and keeps the mind active and curious.

Benefits of Lifelong Learning and Hobbies:

1. MENTAL STIMULATION:

Continuous learning challenges the brain and promotes cognitive health. It enhances memory, problem-solving skills, and creativity.

2. Personal Growth:

Lifelong learning fosters personal growth and self-improvement. It provides opportunities to acquire new skills, knowledge, and perspectives.

3. Sense of Accomplishment:

Pursuing hobbies and learning new things brings a sense of accomplishment and pride. It boosts self-esteem and confidence.

4. Stress Relief:

Engaging in hobbies and learning activities provides a positive outlet for stress relief. It allows for relaxation and enjoyment.

5. Social Interaction:

Learning and hobbies often involve social interactions, whether through classes, clubs, or group activities. These interactions build connections and friendships.

Ways to Engage in Lifelong Learning:

1. Take Classes and Courses:

ENROLL IN CLASSES AND courses to learn new subjects or develop new skills. Many institutions offer courses specifically designed for older adults.

Options for Classes and Courses:

- LOCAL COLLEGES AND Universities: Many colleges and universities offer continuing education programs for older adults. These programs cover a wide range of subjects, from arts and humanities to science and technology.

- Online Courses: Online platforms, such as Coursera, edX, and Khan Academy, provide access to a vast array of courses from the comfort of your home. Topics range from academic subjects to practical skills.

- Community Centers: Community centers and senior centers often offer classes and workshops on various topics, including fitness, arts, technology, and personal development.

2. Join Study Groups and Clubs:

STUDY GROUPS AND CLUBS provide opportunities for collaborative learning and shared interests. They create a supportive environment for exploring new topics.

Examples of Study Groups and Clubs:

- BOOK CLUBS: JOIN A book club to read and discuss books with others. Book clubs offer intellectual stimulation and foster meaningful conversations.

- Language Clubs: Learn a new language or practice language skills in a language club. These clubs provide a fun and social way to enhance language proficiency.

- Science and Technology Groups: Participate in groups that explore scientific and technological topics. These groups keep you updated on new developments and innovations.

3. Explore Online Resources:

THE INTERNET OFFERS a wealth of resources for lifelong learning. Explore websites, videos, and interactive platforms to learn new things at your own pace.

Examples of Online Resources:

- EDUCATIONAL WEBSITES: Visit educational websites, such as TED Talks, National Geographic, or Smithsonian, for informative and inspiring content.

- Virtual Tours: Take virtual tours of museums, historical sites, and cultural landmarks. Virtual tours provide immersive learning experiences from anywhere in the world.

- Podcasts and Webinars: Listen to podcasts and attend webinars on topics of interest. These formats offer convenient and engaging ways to learn.

Pursuing Hobbies and Interests:

1. Identify Your Interests:

REFLECT ON YOUR INTERESTS and passions to identify hobbies that bring you joy and fulfillment. Consider activities you have always wanted to try or skills you want to develop.

Steps to Identify Your Interests:

- REFLECT ON PAST ENJOYMENT: Think about activities you have enjoyed in the past, whether in childhood, adolescence, or adulthood. Revisit hobbies that brought you happiness.

- Explore New Activities: Be open to exploring new activities and interests. Try different hobbies to discover what resonates with you.

- Consider Your Skills: Consider your skills and talents when choosing hobbies. Pursuing activities that align with your strengths can enhance enjoyment and success.

2. Dedicate Time to Hobbies:

MAKE TIME FOR HOBBIES in your daily or weekly schedule. Regularly engaging in activities you love contributes to overall well-being and satisfaction.

Steps to Dedicate Time to Hobbies:

- SCHEDULE HOBBY TIME: Set aside specific times for hobbies in your schedule. Treat this time as an important commitment to yourself.

- Create a Dedicated Space: Designate a space in your home for your hobbies. Having a dedicated space helps you stay organized and focused.

- Stay Consistent: Consistency is key to developing and enjoying hobbies. Make a habit of regularly engaging in your chosen activities.

3. Join Hobby Groups and Classes:

JOINING HOBBY GROUPS and classes provides opportunities to learn from others, share experiences, and build connections.

Examples of Hobby Groups and Classes:

- ART CLASSES: ENROLL in art classes to learn painting, drawing, sculpture, or other visual arts. Art classes foster creativity and self-expression.

- Music Groups: Join music groups, such as choirs, bands, or orchestras, to play an instrument or sing with others. Music groups provide a collaborative and enjoyable way to make music.

- Craft Workshops: Participate in craft workshops to learn skills such as knitting, woodworking, pottery, or jewelry making. Craft workshops offer hands-on learning and creativity.

4. Attend Workshops and Events:

ATTEND WORKSHOPS, EVENTS, and expos related to your hobbies and interests. These gatherings provide inspiration, knowledge, and opportunities to connect with like-minded individuals.

Examples of Workshops and Events:

- CRAFT FAIRS: VISIT craft fairs to explore handmade items, learn new techniques, and connect with artisans.

- Music Festivals: Attend music festivals to enjoy live performances, discover new artists, and celebrate music with others.

- Literary Events: Participate in literary events, such as author readings, writing workshops, or poetry slams, to immerse yourself in the world of literature.

Case Studies: Staying Active and Engaged

Case Study 1: Mary's Journey to Lifelong Learning and Social Connection

Mary, a 68-year-old retired librarian, found joy and fulfillment through lifelong learning and social activities.

Mary's Strategies:

- TAKING CLASSES: MARY enrolled in continuing education courses at a local college, studying subjects such as history, literature, and art. These classes provided mental stimulation and personal growth.

- Joining Clubs: Mary joined a book club and a gardening club. These clubs allowed her to share her interests, engage in meaningful conversations, and build friendships.

- Volunteering: Mary volunteered at a local library, organizing events and helping with community programs. Volunteering gave her a sense of purpose and connection.

- Exploring Online Resources: Mary explored online resources, such as virtual museum tours and educational websites. These resources expanded her knowledge and provided enjoyable learning experiences.

Results:

Through her commitment to lifelong learning and social connection, Mary experienced enhanced mental stimulation, personal growth, and emotional well-being. Mary's journey highlighted the importance of staying active and engaged through continuous learning and community involvement.

Case Study 2: Tom's Path to Physical and Social Engagement

TOM, A 70-YEAR-OLD retired engineer, found fulfillment through physical activity and social engagement.

Tom's Strategies:

- CREATING A FITNESS Routine: Tom created a fitness routine that included walking, swimming, and strength training. He set realistic goals and tracked his progress to stay motivated.

- Joining Sports Clubs: Tom joined a local tennis club and a cycling group. These clubs provided opportunities for physical activity, competition, and social interaction.

- Participating in Community Events: Tom participated in community events, such as charity runs and recreational sports leagues. These events allowed him to stay active and connect with others.

- Volunteering: Tom volunteered as a coach for a youth sports team, sharing his passion for sports and mentoring young athletes. Volunteering gave him a sense of purpose and satisfaction.

Results:

Through his dedication to physical activity and social engagement, Tom enjoyed improved physical health, enhanced social connections, and a fulfilling lifestyle. Tom's path demonstrated the benefits of staying active and involved in the community.

Conclusion

Staying active and engaged is essential for maintaining health, vitality, and overall well-being as we age. By incorporating regular physical activity, participating in social activities and community involvement, and pursuing lifelong learning and hobbies, you can enjoy a fulfilling and enriched life.

In this chapter, we explored the benefits of staying physically active, provided practical tips for incorporating exercise into daily life, highlighted ways to stay socially active and involved in the community, and discussed the importance of lifelong learning and pursuing hobbies. By integrating these practices into your daily routine, you can achieve better health outcomes, enhance your quality of life, and enjoy a vibrant and fulfilling aging experience.

As you continue to explore the strategies for mind, body, and spirit outlined in this book, remember that staying active and engaged is a crucial aspect of living your best life at any age. Embrace the journey of aging with a proactive and positive attitude, and prioritize your physical, social, and intellectual well-being to enjoy a long, healthy, and fulfilling life.

Chapter 10: Nutrition for Longevity

Nutritional Needs of Older Adults

As we age, our nutritional needs change. Understanding these changes is crucial for maintaining health, vitality, and longevity. Proper nutrition can help manage chronic conditions, boost the immune system, and improve overall quality of life. This chapter explores the specific nutritional needs of older adults, highlights superfoods and supplements beneficial for aging well, and provides practical tips for healthy eating habits and meal planning.

Understanding Nutritional Changes with Age:

1. METABOLISM SLOWS Down:

As we age, our metabolism naturally slows down, which means our bodies require fewer calories. However, the need for essential nutrients remains the same or even increases. This necessitates a focus on nutrient-dense foods to meet nutritional requirements without excessive calorie intake.

2. Decreased Appetite:

Many older adults experience a decrease in appetite, which can be due to various factors such as changes in taste and smell, medications, or underlying health conditions. It's important to find ways to stimulate appetite and ensure adequate nutrient intake.

3. Digestive Changes:

Aging can affect digestion and nutrient absorption. Conditions like constipation, decreased stomach acid production, and slower digestive motility are common. Consuming high-fiber foods, staying hydrated, and possibly taking digestive aids can help.

4. Bone Health:

Bone density decreases with age, increasing the risk of osteoporosis and fractures. Adequate intake of calcium and vitamin D is crucial for maintaining bone health.

5. Muscle Mass:

Muscle mass tends to decline with age, leading to sarcopenia (age-related muscle loss). Protein intake becomes even more important to preserve muscle strength and function.

6. Hydration:

Older adults may have a reduced sense of thirst, making them more susceptible to dehydration. Regular fluid intake is essential to maintain hydration and support bodily functions.

Key Nutrients for Older Adults:

1. PROTEIN:

Protein is essential for maintaining muscle mass, repairing tissues, and supporting the immune system. Older adults should aim for a higher protein intake to combat muscle loss.

Good Sources of Protein:

HI- LEAN MEATS (CHICKEN, turkey)

- Fish and seafood

- Eggs

- Dairy products (milk, yogurt, cheese)

- Legumes (beans, lentils, chickpeas)

- Nuts and seeds

- Tofu and tempeh

2. Calcium and Vitamin D:

CALCIUM AND VITAMIN D are critical for bone health. Vitamin D also plays a role in immune function and muscle health.

Good Sources of Calcium:

- DAIRY PRODUCTS (MILK, cheese, yogurt)

- Leafy green vegetables (kale, spinach, broccoli)

- Fortified foods (orange juice, plant-based milk)

- Tofu and tempeh

- Almonds and sesame seeds

Good Sources of Vitamin D:

- SUNLIGHT EXPOSURE

- Fatty fish (salmon, mackerel, sardines)

- Fortified foods (milk, cereals, orange juice)

- Egg yolks

- Supplements (as recommended by a healthcare provider)

3. Fiber:

Fiber aids in digestion, helps prevent constipation, and supports heart health. Older adults should focus on getting both soluble and insoluble fiber.

Good Sources of Fiber:

- WHOLE GRAINS (OATS, brown rice, whole wheat bread)

- Fruits (apples, berries, pears)

- Vegetables (carrots, broccoli, Brussels sprouts)

- Legumes (beans, lentils)

- Nuts and seeds

4. Healthy Fats:

HEALTHY FATS ARE IMPORTANT for brain health, hormone production, and reducing inflammation. Focus on unsaturated fats and limit saturated and trans fats.

Good Sources of Healthy Fats:

- AVOCADOS

- Nuts and seeds

- Olive oil and other plant-based oils

- Fatty fish (salmon, trout, sardines)

- Flaxseeds and chia seeds

5. Vitamins and Minerals:

ADEQUATE INTAKE OF vitamins and minerals is crucial for overall health. Vitamins such as B12, C, E, and K, and minerals like magnesium, potassium, and zinc are particularly important for older adults.

Good Sources of Essential Vitamins and Minerals:

- FRUITS AND VEGETABLES

- Whole grains

- Lean meats and seafood

- Dairy products

- Fortified foods

- Supplements (as recommended by a healthcare provider)

6. Hydration:

Staying hydrated is essential for maintaining body functions, supporting digestion, and preventing dehydration. Older adults should aim for regular fluid intake throughout the day.

Good Sources of Hydration:

- WATER

- Herbal teas

- Broths and soups

- Water-rich fruits and vegetables (cucumbers, watermelon, oranges)

- Low-fat milk and plant-based milk

Superfoods and Supplements for Aging Well

Superfoods are nutrient-dense foods that provide a significant amount of vitamins, minerals, antioxidants, and other beneficial compounds. Incorporating superfoods into your diet can support overall health and help address specific aging-related concerns.

Key Superfoods for Older Adults:

1. BLUEBERRIES:

Blueberries are rich in antioxidants, particularly anthocyanins, which have anti-inflammatory and brain-protective properties. They may help improve cognitive function and reduce the risk of chronic diseases.

Ways to Include Blueberries:

- ADD TO SMOOTHIES OR yogurt

- Sprinkle on cereals or oatmeal

- Enjoy as a snack

2. Leafy Greens:

LEAFY GREENS LIKE SPINACH, kale, and Swiss chard are packed with vitamins (A, C, K), minerals (iron, calcium), and antioxidants. They support bone health, vision, and overall immune function.

Ways to Include Leafy Greens:

- ADD TO SALADS OR SOUPS

- Blend into smoothies

- Sauté as a side dish

3. Salmon:

Salmon is an excellent source of omega-3 fatty acids, which have anti-inflammatory properties and support heart and brain health. It is also rich in high-quality protein and vitamin D.

Ways to Include Salmon:

- GRILL OR BAKE AS A main dish

- Add to salads or sandwiches

- Use in fish tacos or pasta dishes

4. Nuts and Seeds:

NUTS AND SEEDS ARE rich in healthy fats, protein, fiber, vitamins, and minerals. They support heart health, brain function, and overall energy levels.

Ways to Include Nuts and Seeds:

- SNACK ON A HANDFUL of mixed nuts

- Sprinkle seeds on salads, yogurt, or oatmeal

- Use nut butter on toast or in smoothies

5. Greek Yogurt:

GREEK YOGURT IS HIGH in protein, probiotics, and calcium. It supports digestive health, muscle maintenance, and bone strength.

Ways to Include Greek Yogurt:

- ENJOY WITH FRUIT AND honey for breakfast

- Use as a base for smoothies

- Add to savory dishes like soups and sauces

6. Turmeric:

Turmeric contains curcumin, a compound with powerful anti-inflammatory and antioxidant effects. It may help reduce inflammation, support joint health, and improve brain function.

Ways to Include Turmeric:

- ADD TO SOUPS, STEWS, and curries

- Blend into smoothies

- Use in golden milk (turmeric latte)

Supplements for Aging Well:

WHILE IT'S BEST TO obtain nutrients from food, supplements can help fill nutritional gaps, especially when dietary intake is insufficient or specific health conditions require it. Always consult with a healthcare provider before starting any new supplement regimen.

1. Multivitamins:

Multivitamins provide a broad range of essential vitamins and minerals. They can help ensure adequate nutrient intake, especially when dietary intake is limited.

2. Calcium and Vitamin D Supplements:

These supplements support bone health and help prevent osteoporosis. They are particularly important for individuals with limited sun exposure or dietary intake.

3. Omega-3 Fatty Acids:

Omega-3 supplements, such as fish oil, provide essential fatty acids that support heart, brain, and joint health. They are beneficial for reducing inflammation and improving cardiovascular function.

4. Probiotics:

Probiotics support digestive health by promoting a healthy balance of gut bacteria. They can help improve digestion, boost the immune system, and prevent gastrointestinal issues.

5. B Vitamins:

B vitamins, particularly B12, are important for energy production, brain function, and red blood cell formation. Older adults may require B12 supplements due to decreased absorption with age.

Healthy Eating Habits and Meal Planning

Establishing healthy eating habits and effective meal planning are crucial for maintaining optimal nutrition and supporting longevity. This section provides practical tips for healthy eating and offers guidance on creating balanced and nutritious meals.

Healthy Eating Habits:

1. Eat a Balanced Diet:

A BALANCED DIET INCLUDES a variety of foods from all food groups, ensuring that you get a wide range of nutrients. Focus on whole, unprocessed foods and limit added sugars, saturated fats, and sodium.

Components of a Balanced Diet:

- FRUITS AND VEGETABLES: Aim for a variety of colors and types to get a range of vitamins, minerals, and antioxidants.

- Whole Grains: Choose whole grains like brown rice, quinoa, oats, and whole wheat bread for added fiber and nutrients.

- Lean Proteins: Include sources of lean protein, such as poultry, fish, beans, and legumes.

- Healthy Fats: Incorporate healthy fats from sources like avocados, nuts, seeds, and olive oil.

- Dairy or Dairy Alternatives: Choose low-fat or fat-free dairy products or fortified plant-based alternatives.

2. Practice Portion Control:

BEING MINDFUL OF PORTION sizes helps prevent overeating and supports weight management. Use smaller plates and bowls, and avoid eating directly from large packages.

Tips for Portion Control:

- MEASURE PORTIONS: Use measuring cups and spoons to accurately measure portions.

- Visual Cues: Use visual cues, such as comparing portion sizes to common objects (e.g., a serving of meat should be the size of a deck of cards).

- Eat Mindfully: Pay attention to hunger and fullness cues, and avoid distractions like TV or smartphones while eating.

3. Stay Hydrated:

PROPER HYDRATION IS essential for overall health and well-being. Drink water throughout the day and limit sugary beverages and excessive caffeine.

Tips for Staying Hydrated:

- CARRY A WATER BOTTLE: Keep a water bottle with you to encourage regular sipping.

- Set Reminders: Set reminders to drink water, especially if you have a tendency to forget.

- Flavor Water: Add natural flavors to water, such as lemon, cucumber, or mint, to make it more appealing.

4. Limit Processed Foods:

PROCESSED FOODS ARE often high in added sugars, unhealthy fats, and sodium. Focus on whole, unprocessed foods to maximize nutrient intake and minimize empty calories.

Tips for Limiting Processed Foods:

- READ LABELS: CHECK food labels for added sugars, sodium, and unhealthy fats. Choose products with minimal ingredients and recognizable components.

- Cook at Home: Prepare meals at home using fresh ingredients to have better control over what goes into your food.

- Choose Healthier Alternatives: Opt for healthier alternatives, such as whole fruits instead of fruit juices, or homemade snacks instead of packaged ones.

5. Plan and Prepare Meals:

MEAL PLANNING AND PREPARATION help ensure that you have nutritious meals readily available, reducing the temptation to make unhealthy food choices.

Steps for Meal Planning and Preparation:

- PLAN AHEAD: PLAN YOUR meals and snacks for the week, considering variety and balance. Make a shopping list based on your meal plan.

- Prep in Advance: Prepare ingredients in advance, such as chopping vegetables, cooking grains, or marinating proteins. This makes it easier to assemble meals quickly.

- Cook in Batches: Cook larger quantities of meals and store leftovers for later use. This saves time and ensures you have healthy options on hand.

Creating Balanced and Nutritious Meals:

1. Breakfast:

START YOUR DAY WITH a nutritious breakfast that includes protein, healthy fats, and whole grains. A balanced breakfast provides energy and supports metabolism.

Healthy Breakfast Ideas:

- GREEK YOGURT PARFAIT: Layer Greek yogurt with fresh berries, granola, and a drizzle of honey.

- Oatmeal: Cook oats with milk or a dairy alternative, and top with sliced bananas, nuts, and a sprinkle of cinnamon.

- Egg and Vegetable Scramble: Scramble eggs with spinach, tomatoes, and bell peppers. Serve with whole grain toast.

2. Lunch:

A balanced lunch should include a mix of protein, fiber, and healthy fats to keep you satisfied and energized throughout the day.

Healthy Lunch Ideas:

- QUINOA SALAD: TOSS cooked quinoa with chickpeas, cherry tomatoes, cucumbers, and a lemon-tahini dressing.

- Turkey and Avocado Wrap: Fill a whole grain tortilla with sliced turkey, avocado, lettuce, and a light spread of hummus.

- Vegetable Soup: Prepare a hearty vegetable soup with a variety of seasonal vegetables, beans, and a flavorful broth.

3. Dinner:

Dinner should be balanced and not overly heavy, incorporating a variety of food groups to round out your daily nutrition.

Healthy Dinner Ideas:

- BAKED SALMON: SERVE baked salmon with a side of roasted sweet potatoes and steamed broccoli.

- Chicken Stir-Fry: Stir-fry chicken with a mix of colorful vegetables and serve over brown rice or quinoa.

- Stuffed Bell Peppers: Fill bell peppers with a mixture of lean ground turkey, brown rice, and diced tomatoes. Top with a sprinkle of cheese and bake.

4. Snacks:

Healthy snacks help maintain energy levels between meals and prevent overeating. Choose nutrient-dense options that provide sustained energy.

Healthy Snack Ideas:

- FRUIT AND NUT MIX: Combine dried fruits like apricots or raisins with nuts and seeds for a portable and nutritious snack.

- Hummus and Veggies: Dip sliced carrots, celery, and bell peppers into hummus for a satisfying and fiber-rich snack.

- Greek Yogurt and Berries: Enjoy a small bowl of Greek yogurt topped with fresh berries and a drizzle of honey.

Special Dietary Considerations:

1. Managing Chronic Conditions:

PROPER NUTRITION IS crucial for managing chronic conditions such as diabetes, hypertension, and heart disease. Tailor your diet to address specific health needs.

Tips for Managing Chronic Conditions:

- DIABETES: FOCUS ON controlling blood sugar levels by choosing low-glycemic foods, balancing carbohydrates with protein and healthy fats, and monitoring portion sizes.

- Hypertension: Reduce sodium intake by avoiding processed foods and using herbs and spices for flavor. Include potassium-rich foods like bananas, sweet potatoes, and leafy greens.

- Heart Disease: Emphasize heart-healthy fats from sources like fish, nuts, and olive oil. Limit saturated and trans fats, and increase fiber intake from whole grains, fruits, and vegetables.

2. Food Allergies and Intolerances:

IF YOU HAVE FOOD ALLERGIES or intolerances, identify and avoid trigger foods while ensuring you get adequate nutrition from alternative sources.

Tips for Managing Food Allergies and Intolerances:

- READ LABELS: CAREFULLY read food labels to identify potential allergens and avoid cross-contamination.

- Seek Alternatives: Find suitable alternatives for common allergens. For example, use almond milk instead of cow's milk, or gluten-free grains instead of wheat.

- Consult a Dietitian: Work with a registered dietitian to develop a balanced diet that meets your nutritional needs while avoiding allergens.

3. Vegetarian and Vegan Diets:

PLANT-BASED DIETS CAN provide all necessary nutrients when properly planned. Focus on a variety of plant foods to ensure balanced nutrition.

Tips for Vegetarian and Vegan Diets:

- PROTEIN SOURCES: INCLUDE a variety of plant-based protein sources, such as beans, lentils, tofu, tempeh, quinoa, and nuts.

- Nutrient-Rich Foods: Ensure adequate intake of essential nutrients like iron, calcium, vitamin B12, and omega-3 fatty acids. Consider fortified foods or supplements as needed.

- Balanced Meals: Create balanced meals with a mix of protein, whole grains, fruits, vegetables, and healthy fats.

Conclusion:

Nutrition plays a pivotal role in promoting longevity and enhancing quality of life as we age. By understanding the specific nutritional needs of older adults, incorporating superfoods and supplements, and adopting healthy eating habits and meal planning strategies, you can support your health and well-being.

In this chapter, we explored the nutritional changes that occur with age, highlighted key nutrients and superfoods beneficial for older adults, and provided practical tips for healthy eating and meal planning. By integrating these practices into your daily routine, you can achieve better health outcomes, prevent chronic conditions, and enjoy a vibrant and fulfilling aging experience.

As you continue to explore the strategies for mind, body, and spirit outlined in this book, remember that proper nutrition is a crucial aspect of living your best life at any age. Embrace the journey of aging with a proactive and positive attitude, and prioritize your nutritional well-being to enjoy a long, healthy, and fulfilling life.

Chapter 11: Managing Chronic Conditions

Common Chronic Conditions in Older Adults

As we age, the likelihood of developing chronic conditions increases. These conditions can significantly impact quality of life, requiring ongoing management and care. Understanding common chronic conditions, their symptoms, and treatment options is essential for effective management and improving overall well-being.

1. Hypertension (High Blood Pressure):

HYPERTENSION IS A COMMON condition where the force of the blood against the artery walls is too high. It often has no symptoms but can lead to serious health problems if left untreated, such as heart disease, stroke, and kidney damage.

Symptoms and Complications:

- OFTEN ASYMPTOMATIC

- Severe hypertension may cause headaches, dizziness, or nosebleeds

- Long-term complications include heart attack, stroke, heart failure, and kidney disease

Management and Treatment:

- REGULAR BLOOD PRESSURE monitoring

- Lifestyle changes (diet, exercise, weight management)

- Medications (diuretics, ACE inhibitors, beta-blockers)

2. Diabetes:

Diabetes is a condition that affects how the body uses blood sugar (glucose). There are two main types: Type 1 (body does not produce insulin) and Type 2 (body does not use insulin properly).

Symptoms and Complications:

- INCREASED THIRST AND urination

- Fatigue

- Blurred vision

- Slow-healing sores

- Complications include heart disease, kidney damage, nerve damage, and eye problems

Management and Treatment:

- BLOOD SUGAR MONITORING

- Healthy diet and regular exercise

- Medications (insulin, oral hypoglycemics)

- Regular check-ups and screenings

3. Arthritis:

Arthritis involves inflammation of the joints, causing pain, stiffness, and reduced movement. The two most common types are osteoarthritis (wear and tear of joints) and rheumatoid arthritis (autoimmune disease affecting the joints).

Symptoms and Complications:

- JOINT PAIN, SWELLING, and stiffness

- Decreased range of motion

- Chronic pain can lead to decreased mobility and quality of life

Management and Treatment:

- PHYSICAL THERAPY AND exercise

- Weight management

- Medications (NSAIDs, corticosteroids, disease-modifying antirheumatic drugs)

- Joint injections or surgery in severe cases

4. Chronic Obstructive Pulmonary Disease (COPD):

COPD IS A GROUP OF lung diseases that block airflow and make breathing difficult. It includes emphysema and chronic bronchitis, often caused by long-term exposure to irritating gases or particulate matter, most often from cigarette smoke.

Symptoms and Complications:

- SHORTNESS OF BREATH

- Chronic cough

- Wheezing

- Frequent respiratory infections

- Complications include respiratory infections, heart problems, and lung cancer

Management and Treatment:

- SMOKING CESSATION

- Inhalers and medications (bronchodilators, steroids)

- Pulmonary rehabilitation

- Oxygen therapy

5. Heart Disease:

HEART DISEASE ENCOMPASSES various conditions affecting the heart, including coronary artery disease, heart failure, and arrhythmias. It is the leading cause of death among older adults.

Symptoms and Complications:

- CHEST PAIN (ANGINA)

- Shortness of breath

- Fatigue

- Heart attack and stroke are severe complications

Management and Treatment:

- HEALTHY DIET AND REGULAR exercise

- Medications (statins, beta-blockers, anticoagulants)

- Lifestyle changes (smoking cessation, weight management)

- Surgical procedures (angioplasty, bypass surgery)

6. Osteoporosis:

Osteoporosis is a condition where bones become weak and brittle, increasing the risk of fractures. It is often called a "silent disease" because bone loss occurs without symptoms until a fracture occurs.

Symptoms and Complications:

- OFTEN ASYMPTOMATIC until a fracture occurs

- Back pain

- Loss of height over time

- Stooped posture

Management and Treatment:

- CALCIUM AND VITAMIN D supplementation

- Weight-bearing exercise

- Medications (bisphosphonates, hormone-related therapy)

- Fall prevention strategies

7. Alzheimer's Disease and Dementia:

DEMENTIA IS A GENERAL term for a decline in cognitive function severe enough to interfere with daily life. Alzheimer's disease is the most common type of dementia.

Symptoms and Complications:

- MEMORY LOSS

- Difficulty in thinking and problem-solving

- Changes in mood and behavior

- Progression leads to severe cognitive impairment and dependency

Management and Treatment:

- MEDICATIONS (CHOLINESTERASE inhibitors, memantine)

- Cognitive therapies

- Supportive care and caregiver support

- Lifestyle changes (diet, exercise, mental stimulation)

Strategies for Managing and Living with Chronic Illnesses

Effective management of chronic conditions involves a combination of medical treatment, lifestyle modifications, and emotional support. Adopting a proactive approach to managing these conditions can significantly enhance quality of life.

1. Medical Management:

Regular Monitoring and Check-ups:

- REGULAR MONITORING of symptoms and vital signs (e.g., blood pressure, blood sugar levels) helps in early detection and management of complications.

- Schedule routine check-ups with healthcare providers to adjust treatment plans as needed.

Adherence to Medication:

- FOLLOW PRESCRIBED medication regimens strictly. Set reminders to take medications on time.

- Communicate with healthcare providers about any side effects or concerns regarding medications.

Managing Multiple Conditions:

- COORDINATE CARE AMONG multiple healthcare providers. Ensure all providers are aware of the full range of your conditions and treatments.

- Use a medication management system to keep track of different medications and prevent interactions.

2. Lifestyle Modifications:

Healthy Diet:

- FOCUS ON A BALANCED diet rich in fruits, vegetables, whole grains, lean proteins, and healthy fats.

- Limit intake of processed foods, sugars, and saturated fats.

- For specific conditions like diabetes, follow a diet plan that helps control blood sugar levels.

Regular Physical Activity:

- ENGAGE IN REGULAR exercise tailored to your abilities and medical conditions. Activities like walking, swimming, and yoga can be beneficial.

- Exercise helps manage weight, improve cardiovascular health, and enhance overall well-being.

Weight Management:

- MAINTAIN A HEALTHY weight to reduce strain on the heart, joints, and overall body.

- Combine a healthy diet with regular exercise for effective weight management.

Smoking Cessation:

- IF YOU SMOKE, SEEK resources to help quit. Smoking exacerbates many chronic conditions, including heart disease and COPD.

Stress Management:

- PRACTICE STRESS-REDUCING techniques such as meditation, deep breathing exercises, and mindfulness.

- Engage in hobbies and activities that bring joy and relaxation.

3. Emotional and Psychological Support:

Counseling and Therapy:

- CONSIDER COUNSELING or therapy to address the emotional and psychological impact of living with a chronic condition.

- Cognitive-behavioral therapy (CBT) can help manage anxiety, depression, and stress related to chronic illnesses.

Support Groups:

- JOIN SUPPORT GROUPS for individuals with similar conditions. Sharing experiences and advice can provide emotional support and practical tips.

- Support groups can be found through healthcare providers, community centers, and online platforms.

Caregiver Support:

- IF YOU ARE A CAREGIVER, seek support to manage the physical and emotional demands of caregiving.

- Utilize respite care services to take breaks and prevent burnout.

4. Developing a Care Plan:

Collaborate with Healthcare Providers:

- WORK WITH YOUR HEALTHCARE team to develop a comprehensive care plan that addresses all aspects of your condition.

- Include strategies for managing symptoms, medication schedules, dietary guidelines, and physical activity plans.

Set Realistic Goals:

- SET ACHIEVABLE GOALS for managing your condition and improving your quality of life.

- Track your progress and celebrate small victories to stay motivated.

Prepare for Emergencies:

- HAVE A PLAN IN PLACE for medical emergencies. Keep a list of emergency contacts, medications, and important medical information readily accessible.

- Educate family members and caregivers about your condition and emergency procedures.

The Role of Medication and Alternative Therapies

Medications play a critical role in managing chronic conditions, but they are often most effective when combined with alternative therapies and lifestyle changes. Understanding the role of medication and exploring complementary therapies can enhance overall management and well-being.

Medication Management:

1. UNDERSTANDING MEDICATIONS:

- Learn about the medications you are taking, including their purpose, dosage, potential side effects, and interactions with other drugs.

- Use resources like medication guides, pharmacy consultations, and online tools to stay informed.

2. Adherence and Compliance:

- Adhering to prescribed medication regimens is crucial for managing chronic conditions effectively. Use pill organizers, alarms, and reminder apps to help remember doses.

- Discuss any challenges with your healthcare provider, such as difficulty swallowing pills or financial constraints, to find solutions.

3. Managing Side Effects:

- Report any side effects to your healthcare provider. They may adjust the dosage, switch medications, or suggest ways to manage side effects.

- Keep a symptom diary to track side effects and identify any patterns or triggers.

4. Avoiding Medication Interactions:

- Inform your healthcare providers about all medications, supplements, and over-the-counter drugs you are taking to avoid harmful interactions.

- Use a single pharmacy for all prescriptions when possible, so the pharmacist can monitor for potential interactions.

Alternative Therapies:

1. PHYSICAL THERAPIES:

- **Physical Therapy:** Physical therapists can design personalized exercise programs to improve mobility, strength, and function. They can also provide pain relief techniques.

- Occupational Therapy: Occupational therapists help with daily activities and suggest modifications to make tasks easier and safer.

- Massage Therapy: Massage can relieve muscle tension, reduce stress, and improve circulation. It can be particularly beneficial for conditions like arthritis and fibromyalgia.

2. Mind-Body Therapies:

- Meditation and Mindfulness: Practices like meditation, mindfulness, and deep breathing exercises can reduce stress, improve mental clarity, and enhance emotional well-being.

- Yoga and Tai Chi: These gentle, low-impact exercises improve flexibility, balance, and overall physical and mental health. They are particularly beneficial for older adults.

3. Nutritional and Herbal Supplements:

- Omega-3 Fatty Acids: Found in fish oil, omega-3 supplements support heart health and reduce inflammation.

- Turmeric and Curcumin: Known for their anti-inflammatory properties, these supplements can help manage conditions like arthritis.

- Probiotics: Beneficial for digestive health, probiotics support a healthy gut microbiome and can improve overall well-being.

4. Acupuncture:

- Acupuncture involves inserting thin needles into specific points on the body to relieve pain and promote healing. It can be effective for managing chronic pain, arthritis, and other conditions.

5. Chiropractic Care:

- Chiropractic care focuses on diagnosing and treating musculoskeletal disorders, particularly those related to the spine. It can be beneficial for managing back pain, headaches, and joint issues.

6. Aromatherapy:

- Aromatherapy uses essential oils to promote relaxation, reduce stress, and improve mood. It can be used through inhalation, massage, or added to baths.

Integrating Conventional and Alternative Therapies:

1. CONSULT WITH HEALTHCARE Providers:

- Always consult with your healthcare providers before starting any new alternative therapies or supplements. They can help ensure that these therapies do not interfere with your existing treatments.

2. Personalized Care Plans:

- Work with your healthcare team to develop a personalized care plan that incorporates both conventional and alternative therapies. This integrative approach can enhance overall health and well-being.

3. Monitor and Adjust:

- Regularly monitor your progress and the effects of both conventional and alternative therapies. Make adjustments as needed to optimize your treatment plan.

Case Studies: Managing Chronic Conditions

Case Study 1: Emily's Journey with Hypertension and Diabetes

Emily, a 72-year-old retiree, has been managing hypertension and Type 2 diabetes for several years. Her proactive approach to managing these chronic conditions has significantly improved her quality of life.

Emily's Strategies:

- REGULAR MONITORING: Emily regularly monitors her blood pressure and blood sugar levels at home. She keeps a log of her readings to share with her healthcare provider during check-ups.

- Healthy Diet: Emily follows a balanced diet rich in whole grains, lean proteins, fruits, and vegetables. She limits her intake of processed foods, sugars, and sodium.

- Physical Activity: Emily incorporates daily walks and yoga sessions into her routine. These activities help manage her weight, improve cardiovascular health, and reduce stress.

- Medication Adherence: Emily takes her prescribed medications for hypertension and diabetes as directed. She uses a pill organizer and sets reminders to ensure she doesn't miss any doses.

- Stress Management: Emily practices mindfulness meditation and deep breathing exercises to manage stress and improve her mental well-being.

- Support Groups: Emily participates in a diabetes support group where she shares experiences and learns from others facing similar challenges.

Results:

Through her proactive approach and commitment to managing her chronic conditions, Emily has maintained stable blood pressure and blood sugar levels. Her overall health and quality of life have improved, allowing her to enjoy her retirement years actively and independently.

Case Study 2: John's Experience with Arthritis and COPD

JOHN, A 68-YEAR-OLD former construction worker, has been living with arthritis and COPD. By combining conventional and alternative therapies, John has found effective ways to manage his symptoms and improve his daily functioning.

John's Strategies:

- MEDICAL MANAGEMENT: John follows his prescribed medication regimen, which includes inhalers for COPD and anti-inflammatory drugs for arthritis. He has regular check-ups with his healthcare providers to monitor his conditions.

- Physical Therapy: John works with a physical therapist to develop a tailored exercise program that includes stretching, strength training, and low-impact aerobic exercises. These exercises help maintain his mobility and reduce joint pain.

- Smoking Cessation: John successfully quit smoking with the help of a smoking cessation program and support from his family. Quitting smoking has significantly improved his COPD symptoms.

- Dietary Changes: John has made dietary changes to include more anti-inflammatory foods like fatty fish, nuts, and leafy greens. He also stays hydrated and limits his intake of processed foods.

- Alternative Therapies: John receives regular acupuncture treatments to relieve pain and improve his overall well-being. He also practices tai chi to enhance his balance and flexibility.

- Support Networks: John attends a local COPD support group and an arthritis self-management program. These groups provide emotional support and practical advice for managing his conditions.

Results:

John's integrated approach to managing his arthritis and COPD has led to significant improvements in his symptoms and quality of life. He experiences less joint pain, better lung function, and increased mobility, allowing him to engage in daily activities with greater ease and enjoyment.

Conclusion

Managing chronic conditions effectively is crucial for maintaining health, vitality, and quality of life as we age. By understanding common chronic conditions, implementing strategies for living well with these illnesses, and integrating conventional and alternative therapies, older adults can take proactive steps to enhance their well-being.

In this chapter, we explored the common chronic conditions affecting older adults, strategies for managing and living with chronic illnesses, and the role of medication and alternative therapies in comprehensive care. By adopting a proactive and integrated approach to managing chronic conditions, you can achieve better health outcomes, prevent complications, and enjoy a fulfilling and enriched aging experience.

As you continue to explore the strategies for mind, body, and spirit outlined in this book, remember that managing chronic conditions is a crucial aspect of living your best life at any age. Embrace the journey of aging with a proactive and positive attitude, and prioritize your health and well-being to enjoy a long, healthy, and fulfilling life.

Chapter 12: Home Safety and Adaptation

Creating a Safe Living Environment

As we age, creating a safe and comfortable living environment becomes increasingly important. Ensuring that our homes are safe helps prevent accidents, reduce the risk of injuries, and supports independent living. This chapter will discuss practical strategies for creating a safe living environment, making home modifications for aging in place, and utilizing assistive devices and technologies to enhance safety and comfort.

Assessing Home Safety:

1. Identify Potential Hazards:

THE FIRST STEP IN CREATING a safe living environment is to identify potential hazards. Conduct a thorough assessment of your home, paying attention to areas that may pose risks.

Common Home Hazards:

- CLUTTER: EXCESSIVE clutter can obstruct pathways and increase the risk of falls. Keep floors clear and remove unnecessary items.

- Loose Rugs and Carpets: Loose rugs and carpets can be tripping hazards. Secure them with non-slip pads or remove them altogether.

- Poor Lighting: Inadequate lighting can make it difficult to see obstacles. Ensure that all areas, especially stairways and entryways, are well-lit.

- Uneven Surfaces: Uneven surfaces, such as thresholds or steps, can cause trips and falls. Smooth out or mark these areas to increase visibility.

- Electrical Cords: Cords stretched across pathways can be tripping hazards. Use cord covers or move cords out of walkways.

2. Implement Fall Prevention Measures:

FALLS ARE A LEADING cause of injury among older adults. Implementing fall prevention measures can significantly reduce the risk of falls.

Fall Prevention Tips:

- INSTALL HANDRAILS: Install handrails on both sides of staircases and in hallways for added support.

- Use Non-Slip Mats: Place non-slip mats in the bathroom, kitchen, and other areas prone to moisture.

- Secure Rugs: Use non-slip pads under rugs to keep them in place.

- Clear Pathways: Ensure that pathways are clear of obstacles and clutter.

- Wear Appropriate Footwear: Wear non-slip, supportive footwear at all times.

3. Enhance Accessibility:

ENHANCING ACCESSIBILITY in the home makes it easier to move around and perform daily activities independently.

Accessibility Improvements:

- WIDEN DOORWAYS: WIDEN doorways to accommodate mobility aids such as wheelchairs or walkers.

- Install Ramps: Install ramps at entrances to eliminate the need for stairs.

- Lower Counters and Shelves: Adjust the height of counters and shelves to make them accessible from a seated position.

- Use Lever Handles: Replace doorknobs with lever handles for easier operation.

Room-by-Room Safety Assessment:

1. Living Room:

THE LIVING ROOM IS a central gathering area that should be safe and comfortable.

Living Room Safety Tips:

- ARRANGE FURNITURE Wisely: Arrange furniture to create clear pathways and avoid obstructing movement.

- Secure Rugs: Ensure that rugs are securely fastened to prevent slipping.

- Install Grab Bars: Install grab bars near seating areas for support when getting up or sitting down.

- Keep Electrical Cords Tidy: Use cord covers to keep electrical cords out of walkways.

2. Kitchen:

The kitchen is a high-traffic area where safety is paramount, especially when handling hot appliances and sharp objects.

Kitchen Safety Tips:

- USE NON-SLIP MATS: Place non-slip mats in front of the sink and stove.

- Store Frequently Used Items: Store frequently used items within easy reach to avoid overreaching or using step stools.

- Install Proper Lighting: Ensure that the kitchen is well-lit, particularly work areas.

- Use Automatic Shut-Off Appliances: Use appliances with automatic shut-off features to prevent accidents.

3. Bathroom:

The bathroom is a common area for falls due to wet surfaces and limited space.

Bathroom Safety Tips:

- INSTALL GRAB BARS: Install grab bars near the toilet, shower, and bathtub for support.

- Use a Shower Chair: Use a shower chair or bench for added stability while bathing.

- Place Non-Slip Mats: Place non-slip mats in the shower, bathtub, and bathroom floor.

- Elevate the Toilet Seat: Use an elevated toilet seat to make sitting and standing easier.

4. Bedroom:

The bedroom should be a safe and restful space, with easy access to essential items.

Bedroom Safety Tips:

- PLACE A LAMP WITHIN Reach: Keep a lamp or light switch within easy reach of the bed.

- Install Bed Rails: Consider installing bed rails for added support when getting in and out of bed.

- Keep Pathways Clear: Ensure that pathways to the bathroom and door are clear of obstacles.

- Use a Nightlight: Use a nightlight to illuminate the path to the bathroom at night.

5. Stairways:

Stairways can be particularly hazardous if not properly maintained and equipped.

Stairway Safety Tips:

- INSTALL HANDRAILS: Install handrails on both sides of the staircase for support.

- Ensure Proper Lighting: Ensure that stairways are well-lit, with light switches at both the top and bottom.

- Mark Steps: Use contrasting tape to mark the edges of steps for better visibility.

- Keep Stairs Clear: Keep stairways free of clutter and obstacles.

Home Modifications for Aging in Place

Aging in place refers to the ability to live independently in one's own home for as long as possible. Home modifications can make this goal more achievable by addressing mobility, accessibility, and safety concerns.

Key Home Modifications:

1. Entryway and Exterior:

THE ENTRYWAY IS THE first point of access to the home and should be safe and accessible.

Entryway Modifications:

- INSTALL RAMPS: INSTALL ramps to eliminate steps and provide smooth access for wheelchairs or walkers.

- Use Non-Slip Surfaces: Apply non-slip coatings to outdoor steps and walkways.

- Ensure Proper Lighting: Install motion-sensor lights at entryways to improve visibility at night.

- Widen Doorways: Widen doorways to at least 32 inches to accommodate mobility aids.

2. Bathroom:

The bathroom is a key area for modifications to enhance safety and accessibility.

Bathroom Modifications:

- INSTALL A WALK-IN Shower: Replace the bathtub with a walk-in shower to reduce the risk of tripping.

- Use a Handheld Showerhead: Install a handheld showerhead for easier use while seated.

- Add Grab Bars: Install grab bars near the toilet, shower, and bathtub for added support.

- Raise Toilet Height: Use a raised toilet seat or install a higher toilet to make sitting and standing easier.

3. Kitchen:

The kitchen should be designed for ease of use and safety, especially when handling hot or sharp items.

Kitchen Modifications:

- ADJUST COUNTER HEIGHTS: Lower countertops to a comfortable height for individuals using wheelchairs.

- Use Pull-Out Shelves: Install pull-out shelves and drawers for easier access to items.

- Add Task Lighting: Install task lighting under cabinets to illuminate work areas.

- Use Lever Faucets: Replace traditional faucets with lever faucets for easier operation.

4. Living Room:

THE LIVING ROOM SHOULD be comfortable and accessible for relaxation and socialization.

Living Room Modifications:

- SECURE FURNITURE: Ensure that furniture is stable and won't tip over easily.

- Use Adjustable Seating: Use adjustable seating options that provide adequate support and comfort.

- Install Grab Bars: Install grab bars near seating areas for support when getting up or sitting down.

5. Bedroom:

The bedroom should be a safe and restful space with easy access to essential items.

Bedroom Modifications:

- USE ADJUSTABLE BEDS: Consider using an adjustable bed for easier access and comfort.

- Install Bedside Rails: Install bedside rails for added support when getting in and out of bed.

- Ensure Easy Access: Keep essential items within easy reach, such as a lamp, phone, and water.

6. Stairways:

Stairways can be a significant hazard for older adults, and modifications can help reduce the risk of falls.

Stairway Modifications:

- INSTALL STAIR LIFTS: Consider installing a stair lift for easier and safer access to upper levels.

- Use Non-Slip Treads: Apply non-slip treads to each step to improve traction.

- Ensure Proper Lighting: Install adequate lighting to ensure that each step is clearly visible.

- Install Handrails: Install handrails on both sides of the staircase for support.

Hiring Professionals for Home Modifications:

1. CONSULT WITH AN Occupational Therapist:

Occupational therapists can assess your home and recommend specific modifications based on your needs and abilities.

Benefits of Occupational Therapy Consultations:

- PERSONALIZED RECOMMENDATIONS: Receive tailored advice on modifications that will best support your independence and safety.

- Functional Assessments: Occupational therapists conduct functional assessments to determine how you interact with your environment and identify areas for improvement.

2. Hire Licensed Contractors:

WORK WITH LICENSED contractors who have experience in home modifications for aging in place.

Tips for Hiring Contractors:

- CHECK CREDENTIALS: Verify that the contractor is licensed, insured, and experienced in home modifications for older adults.

- Ask for References: Request references from previous clients to ensure the contractor's reliability and quality of work.

- Get Multiple Quotes: Obtain quotes from several contractors to compare pricing and services.

3. Explore Funding Options:

HOME MODIFICATIONS can be costly, but there are funding options available to help cover expenses.

Funding Options for Home Modifications:

- MEDICAID: SOME STATES offer Medicaid programs that cover the cost of home modifications for eligible individuals.

- Veterans Affairs (VA) Benefits: Veterans may be eligible for home modification grants through the VA.

- Nonprofit Organizations: Various nonprofit organizations offer grants and low-interest loans for home modifications.

- Insurance: Check with your insurance provider to see if your policy covers any home modifications.

Assistive Devices and Technologies

Assistive devices and technologies can greatly enhance the safety, comfort, and independence of older adults. From simple aids to advanced technologies, these tools can help manage daily activities and improve quality of life.

Types of Assistive Devices and Technologies:

1. Mobility Aids:

MOBILITY AIDS HELP individuals move around more easily and safely.

Common Mobility Aids:

- CANES: PROVIDE ADDITIONAL support for walking and balance.

- Walkers: Offer stability and support, especially for those with limited mobility.

- Wheelchairs: Provide mobility for individuals who cannot walk or have limited walking ability.

- Scooters: Electric scooters offer an alternative to wheelchairs for longer distances.

2. Hearing Aids:

HEARING AIDS AMPLIFY sound to help individuals with hearing loss communicate and engage with their environment.

Types of Hearing Aids:

- BEHIND-THE-EAR (BTE): Fit behind the ear and are connected to an earmold inside the ear canal.

- In-the-Ear (ITE): Fit entirely inside the outer ear.

- In-the-Canal (ITC): Fit partly in the ear canal and are less visible.

3. Vision Aids:

VISION AIDS HELP INDIVIDUALS with visual impairments perform daily tasks and navigate their environment.

Common Vision Aids:

- MAGNIFIERS: HANDHELD or stand magnifiers enlarge text and images.

- Reading Glasses: Enhance the ability to read small print.

- Screen Readers: Software that reads text aloud on a computer or mobile device.

4. Communication Aids:

COMMUNICATION AIDS support individuals with speech or language difficulties.

Types of Communication Aids:

- SPEECH GENERATING Devices (SGDs): Electronic devices that produce speech.

- Text-to-Speech Apps: Mobile apps that convert text into spoken words.

- Picture Communication Boards: Boards with images and symbols that help convey messages.

5. Personal Emergency Response Systems (PERS):

PERS DEVICES ALLOW individuals to call for help in an emergency with the press of a button.

Features of PERS Devices:

- WEARABLE DEVICES: Typically worn as a pendant or wristband.

- 24/7 Monitoring: Connect to a monitoring center that provides immediate assistance.

- GPS Tracking: Some devices include GPS tracking for location monitoring.

6. Home Automation and Smart Technologies:

HOME AUTOMATION AND smart technologies enhance convenience, safety, and independence.

Common Home Automation Devices:

- SMART SPEAKERS: VOICE-activated devices that control other smart devices, provide information, and play media.

- Smart Lighting: Lighting systems that can be controlled remotely or set on schedules.

- Smart Thermostats: Thermostats that can be adjusted remotely and learn preferences over time.

- Smart Locks: Locks that can be controlled with a smartphone for keyless entry.

Integrating Assistive Devices and Technologies:

1. Consult with Healthcare Providers:

CONSULT WITH HEALTHCARE providers, such as occupational therapists or audiologists, to determine the most appropriate assistive devices for your needs.

Benefits of Professional Consultation:

- PERSONALIZED RECOMMENDATIONS: Receive tailored advice on devices that best support your independence and safety.

- Training and Support: Healthcare providers can offer training on how to use assistive devices effectively.

2. Evaluate and Choose Devices:

EVALUATE DIFFERENT devices and choose those that best meet your needs and preferences.

Steps to Evaluate Devices:

- RESEARCH OPTIONS: Research different devices and their features. Read reviews and testimonials from other users.

- Try Before You Buy: Whenever possible, try out devices before purchasing to ensure they are comfortable and easy to use.

- Consider Cost and Coverage: Check if the device is covered by insurance or other funding options. Compare prices and consider long-term costs.

3. Train and Practice:

PROPER TRAINING AND practice are essential for effectively using assistive devices.

Training Tips:

- FOLLOW INSTRUCTIONS: Carefully read and follow the manufacturer's instructions for use.

- Practice Regularly: Use the device regularly to become comfortable and proficient.

- Seek Help: If you encounter difficulties, seek help from healthcare providers or device manufacturers.

Case Studies: Home Safety and Adaptation

Case Study 1: Margaret's Home Modifications for Aging in Place

Margaret, an 80-year-old widow, wanted to remain in her home as she aged. She made several modifications to enhance safety and accessibility.

Margaret's Strategies:

- BATHROOM MODIFICATIONS: Margaret installed a walk-in shower with grab bars and a shower chair. She also raised the toilet seat and added non-slip mats.

- Kitchen Adjustments: She lowered countertops and installed pull-out shelves to make kitchen tasks easier. She also used lever faucets for easier operation.

- Living Room Enhancements: Margaret rearranged furniture to create clear pathways and added grab bars near seating areas. She also ensured that electrical cords were neatly tucked away.

- Bedroom Safety: She installed bed rails for added support and kept essential items within easy reach. She also used a nightlight to illuminate the path to the bathroom at night.

- Stairway Modifications: Margaret installed handrails on both sides of the staircase and added non-slip treads to each step. She also used a stair lift for safer access to upper levels.

Results:

Margaret's home modifications significantly improved her safety and independence. She was able to navigate her home more easily and confidently, allowing her to age in place comfortably.

Case Study 2: David's Use of Assistive Devices for Independent Living

DAVID, A 75-YEAR-OLD retired teacher, used various assistive devices to maintain his independence and enhance his quality of life.

David's Strategies:

- MOBILITY AIDS: DAVID used a walker for stability and support when walking. He also had a wheelchair for longer distances and outdoor activities.

- Hearing Aids: He used behind-the-ear hearing aids to improve his hearing and communication. He regularly consulted with an audiologist for adjustments and maintenance.

- Vision Aids: David used reading glasses and a handheld magnifier to read books and newspapers. He also installed a screen reader on his computer for easier access to digital content.

- Communication Aids: He used a speech-generating device to assist with communication, especially when his speech was affected by a health condition.

- Personal Emergency Response System: David wore a PERS device that allowed him to call for help in an emergency. The device provided peace of mind for him and his family.

- Home Automation: He used smart speakers to control lighting, set reminders, and play music. He also installed smart locks for keyless entry and enhanced security.

Results:

David's use of assistive devices enabled him to live independently and safely. The devices improved his mobility, communication, and overall quality of life, allowing him to stay connected and engaged with his community.

Conclusion

Creating a safe living environment, making home modifications for aging in place, and utilizing assistive devices and technologies are essential steps for maintaining independence and enhancing quality of life as we age. By addressing potential hazards, enhancing accessibility, and integrating supportive tools, older adults can enjoy a safe, comfortable, and fulfilling living environment.

In this chapter, we explored practical strategies for creating a safe living environment, key home modifications for aging in place, and the role of assistive devices and technologies in enhancing safety and independence. By implementing these strategies, you can achieve better health outcomes, prevent accidents, and enjoy a vibrant and fulfilling aging experience.

As you continue to explore the strategies for mind, body, and spirit outlined in this book, remember that home safety and adaptation are crucial aspects of living your best life at any age. Embrace the journey of aging with a proactive and positive attitude, and prioritize your living environment to enjoy a long, healthy, and fulfilling life.

Chapter 13: Relationships and Social Networks

Maintaining and Building Relationships

As we age, maintaining and building relationships becomes crucial for emotional well-being and overall quality of life. Strong relationships provide support, companionship, and a sense of belonging. This chapter explores strategies for nurturing existing relationships, building new ones, coping with loss and loneliness, and fostering intergenerational connections.

The Importance of Relationships in Later Life

1. EMOTIONAL SUPPORT:

Relationships provide emotional support, helping us cope with stress, anxiety, and life's challenges. Having someone to talk to and share experiences with can alleviate feelings of isolation and improve mental health.

2. Physical Health Benefits:

Strong social connections are linked to better physical health. Socially active individuals tend to have lower risks of chronic diseases, improved immune function, and longer life expectancy.

3. Mental Stimulation:

Interacting with others stimulates the mind and keeps it active. Engaging in conversations, activities, and shared interests promotes cognitive health and reduces the risk of cognitive decline.

4. Sense of Belonging:

Relationships foster a sense of belonging and community. Feeling connected to others enhances self-esteem, provides purpose, and contributes to overall life satisfaction.

Strategies for Maintaining and Building Relationships

1. Stay Connected with Family and Friends:

MAINTAINING REGULAR contact with family and friends strengthens bonds and provides a support network.

Ways to Stay Connected:

- REGULAR COMMUNICATION: Use phone calls, video chats, and messaging apps to stay in touch with loved ones. Schedule regular catch-up sessions to maintain strong connections.

- Social Media: Use social media platforms to connect with family and friends, share updates, and stay informed about each other's lives.

- Family Gatherings: Plan and participate in family gatherings, such as dinners, holidays, and celebrations. These events provide opportunities to bond and create lasting memories.

- Shared Activities: Engage in activities that you and your loved ones enjoy, such as cooking, gardening, or playing games. Shared experiences strengthen relationships.

2. Join Social and Community Groups:

JOINING SOCIAL AND community groups provides opportunities to meet new people, share interests, and build new relationships.

Types of Social and Community Groups:

- HOBBY GROUPS: JOIN groups that focus on your interests, such as gardening, knitting, painting, or photography. These groups provide a platform to share skills and learn from others.

- Fitness Classes: Participate in fitness classes, such as yoga, tai chi, or dance, to stay active and meet like-minded individuals.

- Clubs and Organizations: Join clubs or organizations, such as book clubs, cultural clubs, or volunteer organizations. These groups offer opportunities for social interaction and community involvement.

- Senior Centers: Visit local senior centers that offer a variety of programs, activities, and events for older adults. Senior centers are excellent places to build friendships and stay socially active.

3. Volunteer and Give Back to the Community:

VOLUNTEERING PROVIDES a sense of purpose, helps you stay engaged, and offers opportunities to build new relationships.

Ways to Volunteer:

- LOCAL ORGANIZATIONS: Volunteer with local organizations, such as food banks, shelters, hospitals, or schools. Find causes that resonate with you and align with your values.

- Community Events: Participate in community events, such as festivals, fairs, or fundraisers. Volunteering at events helps you connect with others and contribute to community spirit.

- Mentorship Programs: Become a mentor for young people or peers. Sharing your knowledge and experience can have a positive impact on others and create lasting connections.

4. Foster Intergenerational Connections:

BUILDING RELATIONSHIPS across different age groups fosters understanding, mutual support, and shared experiences.

Ways to Foster Intergenerational Connections:

- FAMILY ACTIVITIES: Spend time with family members of all ages, from grandchildren to elderly relatives. Participate in activities that everyone enjoys, such as family outings, game nights, or cooking together.

- Community Programs: Get involved in community programs that bring together different generations, such as intergenerational mentoring, gardening projects, or art collaborations.

- Educational Initiatives: Participate in educational initiatives that pair older adults with younger students for tutoring, storytelling, or cultural exchange programs.

5. Develop New Friendships:

MAKING NEW FRIENDS enriches your social network and provides new perspectives and experiences.

Tips for Developing New Friendships:

- BE OPEN AND APPROACHABLE: Be open to meeting new people and approachable in social settings. Smile, make eye contact, and engage in conversations.

- Attend Social Events: Attend social events, such as parties, gatherings, or community activities, where you can meet new people.

- Join Classes and Workshops: Enroll in classes or workshops that interest you. These settings provide opportunities to connect with others who share your interests.

- Follow Up: If you meet someone you connect with, follow up and suggest meeting again. Building friendships requires effort and initiative.

Coping with Loss and Loneliness

LOSS AND LONELINESS are common challenges that many older adults face. Coping with these emotions is essential for maintaining mental and emotional well-being.

Understanding Loss and Loneliness

1. LOSS:

Loss can take many forms, including the death of a loved one, the end of a relationship, or the loss of physical or cognitive abilities. Grieving is a natural response to loss, and it is important to allow yourself to feel and process these emotions.

2. Loneliness:

Loneliness is the feeling of being socially isolated or disconnected. It can occur even when surrounded by others and can have significant impacts on mental and physical health.

Strategies for Coping with Loss

1. Allow Yourself to Grieve:

GRIEVING IS A NATURAL and necessary process. Allow yourself to feel and express your emotions without judgment.

Steps to Allow Yourself to Grieve:

- ACKNOWLEDGE YOUR FEELINGS: Recognize and accept your feelings of sadness, anger, or confusion. It is okay to feel these emotions.

- Express Your Emotions: Find healthy ways to express your emotions, such as talking to a trusted friend, writing in a journal, or engaging in creative activities.

- Seek Support: Reach out to family, friends, or support groups for comfort and understanding. Sharing your feelings with others can provide relief and connection.

2. Create Rituals of Remembrance:

CREATING RITUALS OF remembrance helps honor the memory of a loved one and provides a sense of closure.

Ways to Create Rituals of Remembrance:

- MEMORIAL SERVICES: Participate in or organize a memorial service or ceremony to celebrate the life of a loved one.

- Memory Books: Create a memory book or scrapbook filled with photos, stories, and mementos that remind you of your loved one.

- Anniversary Rituals: Observe special anniversaries or dates with rituals that hold personal significance, such as lighting a candle or visiting a meaningful place.

3. Engage in Meaningful Activities:

ENGAGING IN ACTIVITIES that bring joy and purpose can help shift focus from grief and provide a sense of fulfillment.

Meaningful Activities:

- HOBBIES AND INTERESTS: Pursue hobbies and interests that you enjoy and find fulfilling. These activities can provide distraction and satisfaction.

- Volunteer Work: Volunteering offers a sense of purpose and the opportunity to make a positive impact on others.

- Physical Activity: Regular exercise, such as walking, yoga, or swimming, can improve mood and overall well-being.

Strategies for Coping with Loneliness

1. Reach Out to Others:

MAKING AN EFFORT TO reach out to others can help alleviate feelings of loneliness and build connections.

Ways to Reach Out:

- CONTACT FAMILY AND Friends: Call, text, or visit family and friends to stay connected. Even brief interactions can make a difference.

- Join Social Groups: Participate in social groups, clubs, or organizations that interest you. These settings provide opportunities to meet new people and build friendships.

- Use Technology: Use technology, such as video calls, social media, and online forums, to stay in touch with loved ones and connect with others.

2. Participate in Community Activities:

COMMUNITY ACTIVITIES provide opportunities to socialize, engage in meaningful activities, and feel a sense of belonging.

Community Activities:

- CLASSES AND WORKSHOPS: Enroll in classes or workshops that interest you. Learning new skills and sharing experiences with others can reduce feelings of loneliness.

- Volunteer Opportunities: Volunteer in your community to meet new people and contribute to a cause you care about.

- Cultural and Recreational Events: Attend cultural and recreational events, such as concerts, art exhibits, or sports events, to engage with your community and enjoy shared experiences.

3. Practice Self-Compassion:

PRACTICING SELF-COMPASSION involves being kind to yourself and acknowledging your feelings without judgment.

Steps to Practice Self-Compassion:

- BE KIND TO YOURSELF: Treat yourself with the same kindness and understanding that you would offer to a friend. Avoid self-criticism and negative self-talk.

- Acknowledge Your Feelings: Recognize and accept your feelings of loneliness without judgment. Understand that it is a common human experience.

- Engage in Self-Care: Prioritize self-care activities that nurture your well-being, such as taking relaxing baths, reading, or spending time in nature.

4. Seek Professional Support:

IF FEELINGS OF LONELINESS or grief become overwhelming, consider seeking professional support from a therapist or counselor.

Benefits of Professional Support:

- EMOTIONAL GUIDANCE: Therapists and counselors provide emotional guidance and coping strategies to help manage feelings of loss and loneliness.

- Safe Space: Professional support offers a safe and non-judgmental space to express your feelings and work through challenges.

- Personalized Strategies: Therapists can help develop personalized strategies to address your unique needs and circumstances.

Importance of Intergenerational Connections

INTERGENERATIONAL CONNECTIONS bring together people of different ages to share experiences, knowledge, and support. These connections offer numerous benefits for both older and younger generations.

Benefits of Intergenerational Connections

1. MUTUAL LEARNING and Growth:

Intergenerational connections provide opportunities for mutual learning and growth. Older adults can share their wisdom, experiences, and skills, while younger generations offer fresh perspectives and new knowledge.

2. Enhanced Social Support:

Building relationships across generations enhances social support networks. Intergenerational connections provide emotional support, companionship, and a sense of belonging.

3. Promotion of Empathy and Understanding:

Interacting with individuals of different ages fosters empathy and understanding. It helps break down stereotypes and promotes respect and appreciation for diverse life experiences.

4. Cognitive and Emotional Stimulation:

Engaging in intergenerational activities stimulates cognitive and emotional health. Conversations, shared activities, and collaborative projects keep the mind active and promote emotional well-being.

Ways to Foster Intergenerational Connections

1. Family Activities:

SPENDING TIME WITH family members of all ages strengthens bonds and creates lasting memories.

Family Activity Ideas:

- FAMILY OUTINGS: PLAN family outings, such as picnics, hikes, or visits to museums, that everyone can enjoy together.

- Game Nights: Organize family game nights with board games, card games, or interactive video games that appeal to all age groups.

- Storytelling Sessions: Share family stories and experiences, allowing older family members to pass down their knowledge and memories to younger generations.

2. Community Programs:

PARTICIPATE IN COMMUNITY programs that promote intergenerational engagement and collaboration.

Community Program Ideas:

- INTERGENERATIONAL Mentoring: Join programs that pair older adults with young people for mentoring and skill-sharing. Older adults can offer guidance and support, while younger individuals can provide fresh perspectives.

- Gardening Projects: Participate in community gardening projects that bring together people of all ages to grow and maintain gardens. These projects promote teamwork, learning, and environmental stewardship.

- Art and Music Collaborations: Engage in intergenerational art and music projects, such as creating murals, performing in community bands, or participating in art workshops.

3. Educational Initiatives:

EDUCATIONAL INITIATIVES that involve both older and younger generations foster learning, collaboration, and mutual respect.

Educational Initiative Ideas:

- TUTORING PROGRAMS: Participate in tutoring programs that pair older adults with students for academic support and mentorship.

- Cultural Exchange Programs: Join cultural exchange programs that bring together individuals from different generations to share traditions, languages, and cultural practices.

- Technology Workshops: Attend technology workshops where older adults can learn digital skills from younger individuals, promoting digital literacy and bridging the generation gap.

4. Volunteering Together:

VOLUNTEERING ALONGSIDE individuals of different ages fosters camaraderie, shared purpose, and community involvement.

Volunteering Ideas:

- COMMUNITY CLEAN-UP: Participate in community clean-up events that involve people of all ages working together to beautify public spaces.

- Charity Events: Volunteer at charity events, such as food drives, fundraisers, or charity walks, that bring together diverse age groups for a common cause.

- Intergenerational Service Projects: Engage in service projects that involve collaboration between different generations, such as building homes for those in need or organizing community festivals.

Case Studies: Relationships and Social Networks

Case Study 1: Alice's Journey of Building New Friendships

Alice, a 70-year-old retired nurse, moved to a new city after her husband's passing. She was determined to build new relationships and stay socially active.

Alice's Strategies:

- JOINING SOCIAL GROUPS: Alice joined a local book club and a gardening group to meet new people and share her interests. These groups provided a platform for meaningful connections.

- Volunteering: Alice volunteered at a nearby hospital, offering her nursing skills and experience to support patients and staff. Volunteering gave her a sense of purpose and allowed her to meet like-minded individuals.

- Community Involvement: Alice participated in community events, such as farmers' markets, art fairs, and cultural festivals. These events provided opportunities to socialize and feel connected to her new community.

- Using Technology: Alice used social media and video calls to stay in touch with family and friends from her previous hometown. She also joined online forums related to her hobbies, where she connected with people who shared her passions.

Results:

Through her proactive efforts, Alice successfully built a new social network and found companionship in her new city. Her involvement in social groups, volunteering, and community activities enriched her life and provided emotional support.

Case Study 2: Robert's Experience with Intergenerational Connections

ROBERT, A 75-YEAR-OLD retired teacher, found joy and fulfillment through intergenerational connections with his grandchildren and community programs.

Robert's Strategies:

- FAMILY ACTIVITIES: Robert spent quality time with his grandchildren, participating in activities they enjoyed, such as fishing, playing board games, and storytelling. These shared experiences strengthened family bonds.

- Intergenerational Mentoring: Robert joined a mentoring program that paired older adults with high school students. He offered academic support and career advice, while the students taught him about technology and current trends.

- Community Projects: Robert participated in community gardening projects that involved people of all ages. Working together in the garden fostered teamwork, learning, and mutual respect.

- Educational Initiatives: Robert volunteered at a local elementary school, reading to students and helping with classroom activities. His presence and stories enriched the students' learning experiences and bridged the generation gap.

Results:

Robert's involvement in intergenerational activities provided him with a sense of purpose, cognitive stimulation, and emotional fulfillment. The connections he built with younger generations enriched his life and promoted a sense of community.

Conclusion

Maintaining and building relationships, coping with loss and loneliness, and fostering intergenerational connections are essential for emotional well-being and overall quality of life as we age. By nurturing existing relationships, building new ones, and engaging in meaningful activities, older adults can enjoy a vibrant and fulfilling life.

In this chapter, we explored strategies for maintaining and building relationships, coping with loss and loneliness, and fostering intergenerational connections. By implementing these strategies, you can enhance your social support network, find emotional fulfillment, and experience the joy of meaningful connections.

As you continue to explore the strategies for mind, body, and spirit outlined in this book, remember that relationships and social networks are crucial aspects of living your best life at any age. Embrace the journey of aging with a proactive and positive attitude, and prioritize your social well-being to enjoy a long, healthy, and fulfilling life.

Chapter 14: Preparing for End-of-Life

Advanced Care Planning and Palliative Care

Preparing for the end of life is a deeply personal journey that involves making important decisions about medical care, emotional support, and spiritual well-being. This chapter explores the significance of advanced care planning, the role of palliative care, and the importance of having open conversations about death and dying. Additionally, it discusses the emotional and spiritual support necessary during this crucial time.

Understanding Advanced Care Planning

ADVANCED CARE PLANNING involves making decisions about the medical care you would want to receive if you become unable to speak for yourself. It ensures that your preferences and values are honored, providing peace of mind for you and your loved ones.

Key Components of Advanced Care Planning

1. Advance Directives:

ADVANCE DIRECTIVES are legal documents that outline your preferences for medical treatment and appoint someone to make healthcare decisions on your behalf if you are unable to do so.

Types of Advance Directives:

- LIVING WILL: A LIVING will specifies the types of medical treatment you want or do not want if you are terminally ill or in a permanent unconscious state. It may include preferences for life-sustaining treatments, such as resuscitation, mechanical ventilation, and tube feeding.

- Durable Power of Attorney for Healthcare: This document designates a healthcare proxy or agent to make medical decisions on your behalf if you are incapacitated. Choose someone you trust to act in accordance with your wishes.

2. POLST (Physician Orders for Life-Sustaining Treatment):

POLST FORMS ARE MEDICAL orders that indicate your preferences for life-sustaining treatments. They are typically used for individuals with serious illnesses or frailty and provide specific instructions for emergency and end-of-life care.

Components of POLST Forms:

- CPR (CARDIOPULMONARY Resuscitation): Indicates whether you want to receive CPR if your heart stops beating.

- Medical Interventions: Specifies the level of medical intervention you prefer, ranging from full treatment to comfort measures only.

- Artificial Nutrition and Hydration: Indicates whether you want to receive artificial nutrition and hydration if you are unable to eat or drink.

3. Healthcare Proxy and Decision-Making:

APPOINTING A HEALTHCARE proxy ensures that someone you trust can make medical decisions on your behalf if you are unable to do so. This person should be familiar with your values, preferences, and advance directives.

Steps to Appoint a Healthcare Proxy:

- CHOOSE A TRUSTED INDIVIDUAL: Select someone who understands your values and is willing to advocate for your wishes. This person should be able to handle complex medical decisions under pressure.

- Discuss Your Wishes: Have a detailed conversation with your healthcare proxy about your preferences for medical treatment and end-of-life care. Ensure they understand and are committed to honoring your wishes.

- Formalize the Appointment: Complete the necessary legal documents to designate your healthcare proxy. Ensure that your healthcare providers and loved ones have copies of these documents.

Benefits of Advanced Care Planning:

- ENSURES YOUR WISHES Are Honored: Advanced care planning ensures that your preferences for medical treatment are respected, even if you cannot communicate them.

- Reduces Stress for Loved Ones: Having clear instructions in place reduces the burden on family members and loved ones, who may otherwise have to make difficult decisions without knowing your wishes.

- Provides Peace of Mind: Knowing that your healthcare decisions are planned and documented provides peace of mind for you and your loved ones.

The Role of Palliative Care

PALLIATIVE CARE FOCUSES on providing relief from the symptoms and stress of serious illness. It aims to improve quality of life for both the patient and their family, addressing physical, emotional, social, and spiritual needs.

Understanding Palliative Care:

1. Goals of Palliative Care:

PALLIATIVE CARE AIMS to enhance quality of life by managing symptoms, providing emotional support, and addressing the holistic needs of patients and their families.

Key Goals:

- SYMPTOM MANAGEMENT: Alleviate symptoms such as pain, nausea, shortness of breath, and fatigue.

- Emotional Support: Provide counseling and support for patients and families coping with the emotional impact of serious illness.

- Coordination of Care: Coordinate care among different healthcare providers to ensure comprehensive and consistent treatment.

- Advance Care Planning: Assist with advance care planning and decision-making to ensure that patients' preferences are honored.

2. Who Provides Palliative Care:

PALLIATIVE CARE IS provided by a multidisciplinary team of healthcare professionals, including doctors, nurses, social workers, chaplains, and other specialists.

Team Members and Their Roles:

- PHYSICIANS: OVERSEE medical treatment and symptom management, and coordinate care with other providers.

- Nurses: Provide hands-on care, monitor symptoms, and educate patients and families about managing illness.

- Social Workers: Offer counseling, support, and assistance with accessing resources and services.

- Chaplains: Provide spiritual support and address the spiritual needs and concerns of patients and families.

- Other Specialists: May include physical therapists, nutritionists, and pharmacists who contribute to comprehensive care.

3. When to Consider Palliative Care:

PALLIATIVE CARE CAN be introduced at any stage of a serious illness, alongside curative treatments. It is not limited to end-of-life care and can be provided in various settings, including hospitals, nursing homes, and patients' homes.

Indications for Palliative Care:

- CHRONIC ILLNESSES: Conditions such as heart disease, cancer, chronic obstructive pulmonary disease (COPD), kidney failure, and neurological disorders.

- Symptom Burden: Severe or persistent symptoms that impact quality of life and daily functioning.

- Emotional and Spiritual Distress: Patients and families experiencing emotional, social, or spiritual challenges related to illness.

- Complex Medical Needs: Situations requiring coordinated care among multiple healthcare providers and specialists.

Conversations About Death and Dying

HAVING CONVERSATIONS about death and dying can be difficult, but they are essential for ensuring that your wishes are known and respected. Open and honest communication with loved ones and healthcare providers can help ease the emotional burden and facilitate meaningful end-of-life planning.

Initiating Conversations About Death and Dying:

1. Overcoming Barriers:

FEAR, DISCOMFORT, AND cultural taboos can make conversations about death challenging. Acknowledging these barriers and approaching the topic with sensitivity can facilitate meaningful discussions.

Common Barriers and Strategies to Overcome Them:

- FEAR OF CAUSING DISTRESS: Concerns about upsetting loved ones can hinder conversations. Emphasize the importance of discussing your wishes to provide clarity and peace of mind.

- Denial: Some individuals may avoid discussing death due to denial or fear. Gently introduce the topic and provide reassurance that it is a natural and important part of life.

- Cultural Taboos: Cultural beliefs and traditions may influence attitudes toward discussing death. Respect cultural sensitivities while emphasizing the value of open communication.

2. Choosing the Right Time and Place:

SELECT A COMFORTABLE and private setting for conversations about death and dying. Choose a time when everyone involved can participate without distractions.

Tips for Choosing the Right Time and Place:

- PLAN AHEAD: SCHEDULE a time when you and your loved ones can have an uninterrupted and focused conversation.

- Create a Comfortable Environment: Choose a quiet, comfortable setting where everyone feels at ease. Ensure privacy and minimize distractions.

- Be Patient: Allow time for the conversation to unfold naturally. Be prepared for multiple discussions over time rather than trying to cover everything in one session.

3. Using Conversation Starters:

USING CONVERSATION starters can help initiate discussions about end-of-life preferences and wishes.

Examples of Conversation Starters:

- REFLECT ON EXPERIENCES: "Remember when [a loved one] went through [an illness or end-of-life experience]? It made me think about what I would want in a similar situation."

- Share Your Thoughts: "I've been thinking about my own wishes for the future, and I'd like to talk about them with you."

- Ask for Input: "Have you thought about what you would want if you were seriously ill or unable to communicate? I'd like to know your thoughts."

Discussing End-of-Life Preferences:

1. Medical Treatment Preferences:

DISCUSS YOUR PREFERENCES for medical treatments, including life-sustaining interventions, resuscitation, mechanical ventilation, and artificial nutrition and hydration.

Topics to Cover:

- LIFE-SUSTAINING TREATMENTS: Do you want to receive treatments such as CPR, mechanical ventilation, or dialysis if they are needed to sustain life?

- Comfort Care: What are your preferences for pain management and comfort measures? Would you prioritize comfort over prolonging life?

- Hospital vs. Home Care: Would you prefer to receive care at home, in a hospital, or in a hospice facility?

2. Personal and Spiritual Wishes:

DISCUSS YOUR PERSONAL and spiritual wishes for end-of-life care, including rituals, religious practices, and meaningful experiences.

Topics to Cover:

- Spiritual Practices: Are there specific religious or spiritual practices you want to be followed at the end of life?

- Rituals and Traditions: Are there cultural or family traditions that are important to you?

- Meaningful Experiences: Are there experiences or activities you want to have or avoid as you approach the end of life?

3. Legacy and Remembrance:

DISCUSS HOW YOU WOULD like to be remembered and any specific wishes for memorial services or legacy projects.

Topics to Cover:

- MEMORIAL SERVICES: Do you have preferences for the type of memorial service, including location, format, and participants?

- Legacy Projects: Are there specific ways you want to be remembered, such as through donations, scholarships, or creative projects?

- Personal Messages: Do you want to leave personal messages or letters for loved ones?

Emotional and Spiritual Support in End-of-Life Care

END-OF-LIFE CARE INVOLVES addressing the emotional and spiritual needs of patients and their families. Providing compassionate support during this time can enhance comfort, peace, and dignity.

Emotional Support:

1. Providing Compassionate Presence:

BEING PRESENT WITH a loved one at the end of life is a powerful way to provide emotional support. Your presence alone can offer comfort and reassurance.

Ways to Provide Compassionate Presence:

- LISTEN ACTIVELY: OFFER a listening ear without judgment. Allow your loved one to express their feelings, fears, and concerns.

- Offer Comforting Touch: Gentle touch, such as holding hands or giving a hug, can provide physical and emotional comfort.

- Create a Calm Environment: Ensure the environment is peaceful and soothing, with soft lighting, calming music, and minimal noise.

2. Facilitating Open Communication:

ENCOURAGE OPEN COMMUNICATION and provide opportunities for your loved one to share their thoughts and feelings.

Tips for Facilitating Open Communication:

- ASK OPEN-ENDED QUESTIONS: Ask questions that invite reflection and discussion, such as "How are you feeling today?" or "Is there anything you want to talk about?"

- Validate Emotions: Acknowledge and validate your loved one's emotions, whether they are feelings of sadness, fear, or anger. Offer empathy and understanding.

- Respect Silence: Allow moments of silence for reflection and processing. Silence can be a powerful form of communication.

3. Offering Practical Support:

PROVIDING PRACTICAL support can alleviate stress and allow your loved one to focus on emotional and spiritual well-being.

Ways to Offer Practical Support:

- ASSIST WITH DAILY Tasks: Help with daily tasks such as meal preparation, housekeeping, and personal care.

- Coordinate Care: Assist with coordinating medical appointments, transportation, and communication with healthcare providers.

- Manage Logistics: Help manage logistics related to advance directives, legal documents, and financial matters.

Spiritual Support:

1. Addressing Spiritual Needs:

SPIRITUAL NEEDS CAN include the search for meaning, connection to a higher power, and the need for peace and reconciliation.

Ways to Address Spiritual Needs:

- FACILITATE SPIRITUAL Practices: Support your loved one's spiritual practices, such as prayer, meditation, or attending religious services.

- Provide Access to Spiritual Leaders: Arrange visits with spiritual leaders, chaplains, or clergy who can offer guidance and support.

- Encourage Reflection: Encourage your loved one to reflect on their life, achievements, and values. Provide a safe space for them to share their thoughts and insights.

2. Creating Meaningful Rituals:

RITUALS CAN PROVIDE comfort, structure, and a sense of continuity during the end-of-life journey.

Examples of Meaningful Rituals:

- DAILY PRAYER OR MEDITATION: Establish a routine of daily prayer or meditation that aligns with your loved one's spiritual beliefs.

- Lighting Candles: Light candles as a symbol of hope, peace, or remembrance.

- Storytelling: Share stories and memories that celebrate your loved one's life and legacy.

3. Promoting Inner Peace and Reconciliation:

HELPING YOUR LOVED one achieve inner peace and reconciliation can provide comfort and closure.

Ways to Promote Inner Peace:

- ENCOURAGE FORGIVENESS: Encourage your loved one to seek forgiveness and offer forgiveness to others. This can bring a sense of resolution and peace.

- Facilitate Closure: Assist your loved one in saying goodbye to friends and family. Encourage meaningful conversations and expressions of love and gratitude.

- Support Emotional Expression: Allow your loved one to express their emotions freely, whether through talking, writing, or creative activities.

Case Studies: Preparing for End-of-Life

Case Study 1: Emma's Journey with Advanced Care Planning

Emma, an 82-year-old woman with advanced heart disease, decided to engage in advanced care planning to ensure her wishes were known and respected.

Emma's Strategies:

- CREATING ADVANCE DIRECTIVES: Emma completed a living will and designated her daughter as her healthcare proxy. She specified her preferences for life-sustaining treatments and comfort measures.

- Discussing Wishes with Family: Emma had a series of conversations with her family to discuss her wishes for end-of-life care, including her preferences for pain management, hospital vs. home care, and spiritual practices.

- Consulting Healthcare Providers: Emma consulted with her healthcare providers to discuss her advance directives and ensure they were documented in her medical records.

- Completing a POLST Form: Given her serious illness, Emma completed a POLST form with her physician to provide specific instructions for emergency and end-of-life care.

Results:

Emma's proactive approach to advanced care planning provided clarity and peace of mind for both her and her family. Her wishes were documented and respected, ensuring that she received the care she desired at the end of her life.

Case Study 2: John's Experience with Palliative Care and Emotional Support

JOHN, A 75-YEAR-OLD man with advanced cancer, received palliative care to manage his symptoms and enhance his quality of life.

John's Strategies:

- ENGAGING IN PALLIATIVE Care: John enrolled in a palliative care program that provided comprehensive support for his physical, emotional, and spiritual needs. His care team included a physician, nurse, social worker, and chaplain.

- Managing Symptoms: The palliative care team focused on managing John's pain, nausea, and fatigue. They adjusted his medications and provided complementary therapies, such as massage and acupuncture.

- Receiving Emotional Support: John received counseling from the palliative care social worker to address his emotional and psychological needs. He also participated in a support group for individuals with advanced cancer.

- Finding Spiritual Comfort: The chaplain provided spiritual support, helping John explore his beliefs, find meaning, and achieve a sense of peace. John also engaged in daily prayer and meditation.

Results:

John's palliative care team provided comprehensive and compassionate support, significantly improving his quality of life. The emotional and spiritual support he received helped him find peace and fulfillment during his final months.

Conclusion

Preparing for end-of-life involves making important decisions about advanced care planning, engaging in palliative care, and providing emotional and spiritual support. By addressing these aspects, individuals can ensure that their wishes are honored, their symptoms are managed, and they experience comfort and dignity during their final journey.

In this chapter, we explored the significance of advanced care planning, the role of palliative care, and the importance of having conversations about death and dying. Additionally, we discussed the emotional and spiritual support necessary for end-of-life care. By implementing these strategies, individuals and their loved ones can navigate the end-of-life journey with compassion, understanding, and peace.

As you continue to explore the strategies for mind, body, and spirit outlined in this book, remember that preparing for end-of-life is a crucial aspect of living your best life at any age. Embrace this journey with a proactive and positive attitude, and prioritize your emotional and spiritual well-being to enjoy a long, healthy, and fulfilling life.

Chapter 15: Conclusion: Living Your Best Life at Any Age

Recap of Key Strategies for Aging Well

As we journey through life, aging is a natural and inevitable process that brings about physical, emotional, and spiritual changes. Throughout this book, we've explored various strategies for aging well, focusing on the mind, body, and spirit. In this concluding chapter, we will recap these key strategies, encourage ongoing growth and adaptation, and share final thoughts on embracing the journey of aging.

Physical Health and Wellness:

1. REGULAR PHYSICAL Activity:

Staying physically active is essential for maintaining strength, flexibility, balance, and cardiovascular health. Engage in activities you enjoy, such as walking, swimming, yoga, or dancing. Aim for at least 150 minutes of moderate-intensity aerobic activity per week, along with muscle-strengthening exercises.

2. Balanced Nutrition:

A well-balanced diet provides the nutrients needed to support overall health. Focus on a variety of fruits, vegetables, whole grains, lean proteins, and healthy fats. Stay hydrated and limit processed foods, added sugars, and unhealthy fats.

3. Preventive Healthcare:

Regular check-ups, screenings, and vaccinations are crucial for early detection and prevention of health issues. Follow your healthcare provider's recommendations for routine exams and screenings based on your age and health history.

4. Managing Chronic Conditions:

If you have chronic conditions, work with your healthcare team to manage them effectively. Adhere to prescribed treatments, monitor your symptoms, and make lifestyle adjustments to improve your quality of life.

Mental Health and Cognitive Wellness:

1. MENTAL STIMULATION:

Keep your mind active through activities that challenge and engage your cognitive abilities. Puzzles, reading, learning new skills, and engaging in creative pursuits can help maintain cognitive function.

2. Stress Management:

Practice stress-reducing techniques such as meditation, deep breathing exercises, and mindfulness. Find activities that bring you joy and relaxation, and make time for them regularly.

3. Emotional Well-Being:

Recognize and address your emotional needs. Build a support network of friends, family, and mental health professionals. Don't hesitate to seek help if you're feeling overwhelmed or experiencing emotional distress.

Social Connections and Relationships:

1. MAINTAINING RELATIONSHIPS:

Nurture existing relationships with family and friends. Stay connected through regular communication, shared activities, and mutual support.

2. Building New Relationships:

Join social and community groups to meet new people and build new friendships. Volunteering, participating in classes, and attending community events are excellent ways to expand your social network.

3. Intergenerational Connections:

Foster relationships across different age groups. Engage in activities that bring together people of all ages, such as family gatherings, community projects, and educational initiatives.

Spiritual Growth and Fulfillment:

1. EXPLORING SPIRITUALITY:

Take time to explore and deepen your spiritual beliefs and practices. Whether through organized religion, meditation, or personal reflection, find what brings you peace and fulfillment.

2. Finding Purpose and Meaning:

Engage in activities that give you a sense of purpose and contribute to your sense of self-worth. Volunteering, mentoring, and pursuing hobbies can provide meaningful engagement.

3. Creating Rituals and Traditions:

Establish rituals and traditions that bring you comfort and joy. These can include daily practices, family traditions, or personal milestones that you celebrate.

Home Safety and Adaptation:

1. CREATING A SAFE Living Environment:

Identify and address potential hazards in your home to prevent accidents and injuries. Implement fall prevention measures, enhance accessibility, and ensure proper lighting.

2. Home Modifications for Aging in Place:

Make modifications to your home to support independence and comfort. Consider installing ramps, grab bars, walk-in showers, and adjustable seating.

3. Utilizing Assistive Devices and Technologies:

Use assistive devices and smart technologies to enhance safety and convenience. Mobility aids, personal emergency response systems, and home automation devices can support independent living.

Preparing for End-of-Life:

1. ADVANCED CARE PLANNING:

Engage in advanced care planning to ensure your wishes are known and respected. Complete advance directives, appoint a healthcare proxy, and discuss your preferences with loved ones.

2. Palliative Care:

Consider palliative care to manage symptoms and improve quality of life if you have a serious illness. Palliative care provides comprehensive support for physical, emotional, and spiritual needs.

3. Conversations About Death and Dying:

Have open and honest conversations about end-of-life preferences with loved ones and healthcare providers. Discuss your wishes for medical treatment, personal and spiritual needs, and legacy.

Encouragement for Ongoing Growth and Adaptation

AGING IS A CONTINUOUS journey that requires ongoing growth, adaptation, and resilience. Embracing this journey with a positive and proactive attitude can lead to a fulfilling and enriched life. Here are some ways to encourage ongoing growth and adaptation:

Embrace Change:

CHANGE IS A NATURAL part of aging. Embrace the changes that come with aging and view them as opportunities for growth and learning. Adapt to new circumstances with flexibility and an open mind.

Set New Goals:

CONTINUOUSLY SET NEW goals and aspirations, regardless of your age. Setting goals gives you a sense of direction and purpose. Whether they are related to health, hobbies, relationships, or personal growth, strive to achieve them.

Learn Continuously:

LIFELONG LEARNING KEEPS your mind active and engaged. Take up new hobbies, attend classes, read widely, and explore new interests. Learning new skills and acquiring knowledge enhances cognitive function and enriches your life.

Stay Positive:

MAINTAIN A POSITIVE outlook on life. Focus on the things you can control and let go of what you cannot. Practice gratitude, celebrate your achievements, and find joy in the small moments.

Practice Self-Compassion:

BE KIND TO YOURSELF and acknowledge your achievements and efforts. Aging can bring challenges, but practicing self-compassion helps you navigate them with grace and resilience.

Stay Connected:

MAINTAIN AND BUILD social connections. Surround yourself with supportive and positive people. Engage in activities that promote social interaction and build a sense of community.

Adapt to New Technologies:

EMBRACE NEW TECHNOLOGIES that can enhance your quality of life. From communication tools to health monitoring devices, technology can provide convenience, safety, and new opportunities for engagement.

Prioritize Self-Care:

TAKE CARE OF YOUR PHYSICAL, emotional, and spiritual well-being. Engage in activities that nourish your body, mind, and soul. Self-care is essential for maintaining overall health and well-being.

Final Thoughts on Embracing the Journey of Aging

AGING IS A UNIQUE AND personal journey that encompasses growth, change, and reflection. Embracing this journey with an open heart and mind allows you to live your best life at any age. Here are some final thoughts on embracing the journey of aging:

Celebrate Your Life:

CELEBRATE YOUR LIFE and the experiences that have shaped you. Reflect on your achievements, lessons learned, and the people who have influenced your journey. Each stage of life is an opportunity for growth and discovery.

Find Joy in the Present Moment:

LIVE IN THE PRESENT moment and find joy in the here and now. Practice mindfulness and appreciate the beauty of everyday life. Cherish the moments of connection, love, and laughter.

Cultivate Resilience:

RESILIENCE IS THE ABILITY to adapt and thrive in the face of challenges. Cultivate resilience by developing coping strategies, seeking support, and maintaining a positive outlook. Resilience helps you navigate the ups and downs of life with strength and grace.

Express Gratitude:

PRACTICE GRATITUDE regularly. Acknowledge the blessings in your life and express appreciation for the people and experiences that bring you joy. Gratitude fosters a sense of contentment and fulfillment.

Nurture Your Spirit:

NURTURE YOUR SPIRIT through activities that bring you peace and fulfillment. Whether through prayer, meditation, nature, or creative expression, find what connects you to your inner self and the world around you.

Leave a Legacy:

CONSIDER THE LEGACY you want to leave behind. Reflect on the values, lessons, and memories you want to pass on to future generations. Your legacy is a testament to the life you have lived and the impact you have made.

Embrace Your Unique Journey:

EMBRACE YOUR UNIQUE journey and honor your individuality. Aging is a personal experience that is shaped by your choices, experiences, and perspectives. Celebrate your uniqueness and live authentically.

Continue to Dream:

CONTINUE TO DREAM AND envision the future. Aging does not mean the end of dreams and aspirations. Allow yourself to dream big, set new goals, and pursue new passions. Your dreams are a reflection of your inner vitality and zest for life.

Conclusion

Living your best life at any age is a journey that encompasses physical health, mental well-being, social connections, spiritual growth, and self-care. By embracing the strategies outlined in this book, you can navigate the aging process with confidence, resilience, and joy.

In this concluding chapter, we recapped key strategies for aging well, encouraged ongoing growth and adaptation, and shared final thoughts on embracing the journey of aging. Remember that aging is a natural part of life, and each stage offers opportunities for growth, learning, and fulfillment.

As you continue on your journey, may you find strength, joy, and peace in every moment. Embrace the changes, celebrate your life, and live each day to the fullest. Aging is not just about getting older; it is about living well, with purpose, passion, and a positive spirit.

Thank you for joining us on this journey. Here's to living your best life at any age.

Don't miss out!

Visit the website below and you can sign up to receive emails whenever Timothy Scott Phillips publishes a new book. There's no charge and no obligation.

https://books2read.com/r/B-A-KCQWC-CUIJF

BOOKS 2 READ

Connecting independent readers to independent writers.

About the Author

Timothy Scott Phillips is a dedicated author specializing in non-fiction self-help books that empower readers to overcome challenges and embrace personal growth. With a passion for mental health, resilience, and self-improvement, Timothy combines research-based insights with practical strategies to inspire lasting change. His work reflects a deep commitment to helping individuals navigate life's complexities, build confidence, and unlock their full potential. When he's not writing, Timothy enjoys mentoring, exploring nature, and connecting with his readers to share stories of transformation and hope. His books are a testament to the power of perseverance and the human spirit.